CH00741130

Losing it in Cornwall

Liz Hurley

Mudlark's Press

Cover artwork "Hilda" by Duane Bryers. Copyright
Brown & Bigelow.

Publisher: Mudlark's Press

ISBN-13: 9780993218019

Dedicated to my long suffering, much maligned family.

With Thanks,

It seems like a complete indulgence to have a section on who I couldn't have done this without. Soon I'll be sobbing and thanking my agent and my muse but then I thought that it was pretty narcissistic to gather together all my witterings in one book and expect people to then read the damn thing anyway. So I think we'll assume that the indulgence part has already been covered.

First off, thank you to the readers of the Cornish Guardian who told me that they had read my column. I don't know if this was praise or sympathy but as I mentioned a minute ago, I'm going to go with the narcissistic option. Secondly, to Helen for telling me I should write a book. I think she meant a novel but as I had already written all these columns I went for them instead. Nothing if not lazy. Then thanks to Al and Simon who felt the project had enough legs to financially back it. Although I declined in case it was a total train wreck and have done it all on a shoestring instead. Add insecure and cheap to my list of virtues. Finally to Anna and Anna who proof read massive sections and helped with the cover design. Those girls are demons at spotting extra spaces, let alone typos and missing commas. Therefore, any mistakes you do spot will be 100% all my own work.

So there we are. I proudly present to you the illiterate ramblings of a vain, lazy, cheap and insecure writer. Enjoy!

Contents Pages

Marmalade Fish

Have you ever made your own marmalade? Tasty, fun and barring explosions, very easy. I'll come back to the explosions in a bit. January is the time to make proper marmalade as it's the Seville orange season. These warty, ugly, sour oranges are only available for a short period so you need to grab them when you see them. Richards by Par docks always has a good supply in and they often have little recipe sheets to go with whatever they have in at the time. Marmalade is one of those wonderful seasonal foods, of course you can make marmalade all year round with lemons and grapefruits and sweet oranges and so on, but for a proper strong, rich marmalade you need the sevilles.

The most tedious part is slicing the rind, and because I need a sharp knife to do it, it's not one of those "fun" tasks I can con the children into doing. Eventually, fingers stinging from the acidic juice, the deed is done and then it's just softening in water and melted sugar and then boiling the whole lot until a set is reached. If you don't pay careful attention and forget to stir regularly you may cause a skin, which may burst in a rather volcanic manner leaving you and the kitchen covered in boiling hot sticky sugar and orange peel. This is not desirable. Providing you have avoided doing this you will have loads of gorgeous jars full of delicious orange marmalade shining back at you. If you line them up on the window they look like captured suns and always make me think of summer, despite the fact that I am making them in the dead of winter, with the wind and the rain lashing around the doors and windows. Even better is to spread some over a thick slice of white bread heavily coated in butter, a coffee by my side, a book in my hand and a fire in the hearth.

Winter seems an obvious time to think about food, all those lovely heartening stews and soups, big roasts, bowls of porridge and whilst I often think of fish as a summer food. I've been thinking about it a lot following the Hugh Fernley-Whittingstall programme on fish discards. I've never seen such criminal waste. One fisherman said "it might not be legally wrong but it is morally wrong" and he was right. I live here by the sea, a huge part of our economy comes from the sea but I was unaware of the senseless waste that our fishermen are being forced to throw away. I know all about tuna issues and farmed salmon but the concept of the quota missed me by completely. I was incensed to see those huge dead fish being thrown back overboard. There was a wonderful Ealing Comedies moment when the fishing fleet threw their "discards" overboard within paddling reach of the shore. Like Whisky Galore the locals made the most of their unusual harvest filleting the lovely free fish and making a feast of it.

The scientists say that the stock levels aren't high enough and I have to respect their opinions as much as the fishermen's, as I don't yet know enough about the subject. But from what I can see, throwing back dead fish is wrong. Maybe like marmalade we need to start thinking more about the season that the food is naturally available in, and the quantities that it's available in, and change our lifestyle accordingly!

Rubenesque is never a compliment

There I was, lying on a muddy rugby pitch doing sit ups looking at the stars; the grass was wet, the muscles were straining and I was very, very tired. What appalling set of circumstances could have conspired to find me doing exercises in the rain on a rugby pitch at 6.15 in the morning? Unfortunately it was nothing less than twenty odd years of fun and excess. Which is why I am at Boot Camp or as our trainer rather unpleasantly calls it "Flab-u-less" I don't know if I object to the –u-, the flab or the pun the most, but I prefer to call it boot camp. Let's call a spade a spade, look each other in the eye and bravely accept that all those years of carousing have finally caught up with us but let's not call it flab. Don't get me wrong, I love me but I'd love a little less of me more.

It all came about when an old friend came to stay; he lives in New Zealand so I only get to see him about once a year. He's a great friend with whom I've spent many years carousing so we're pretty close but he can say things that leave the more sensitive amongst us reeling. We were playing cards and he commented on how Rubenesque I was looking these days. In his defence he was smiling at the time and paying me a compliment. Or so he thought. Oh, the sudden silence and then the screams and the laughter. All the girls were chiding him roundly; the boys were sniggering into their glasses grateful that it was some other chap that had put his foot in it. I was glaring and poor Mark was floundering and apologising but not knowing why. Rubenesque indeed!

Well I was cut to the bone but as the bone was apparently below many Rubenesque layers this cutting took some time. Finally, with a sigh I had to acknowledge that thinking about exercise has far fewer benefits than actually doing it. Although it does have the benefit of you staying warm and dry in bed with no aches. So here I am typing, even that makes me ache, and hoping that this torture will all be for the good. Next week the detox part starts, this fresh hell will involve the removal of coffee and alcohol from my diet which is going to be tricky as they are two of my basic food groups. If Petra also removes sugars and fat then we are in for a pretty hairy month at Chez Hurley but I'm sure she won't, she's seems really nice and friendly.

Now the reason that I'm sharing this with you is so that I can't back out. I'm brilliant at prevarication and just down right laziness but I figure that if I commit myself to print then I'll have to see it through. So we'll speak no more of it and in a month's time I'll let you know if I survived and more importantly if the family survived.

With no wine to recommend all I can suggest is that you pop into Ellis Wharton Wines or del Monico's yourself and ask what they suggest. If you come across something great, please keep it to yourself.

The Glorious Art of the Book

Penguin are currently selling James and the Giant Peach for £100. It's a limited edition hardback designed by Antony Gormley and is one of six titles in a special series. It's hard to tell if it's worth the money, their website only shows you three photos, for £100 I would want close up images of binding, I'd want hand painted or marbled endpapers I'd want to see the quality of the paper and I'd like the designer to sign it. A Perspex slipcase is not enough of a deal breaker for me. Now Penguin may not be showing you the fine details of this book but they are showing you the larger picture of things to come in the publishing world.

In 10 years' time the way you read your book may well have changed completely, so much money is being invested in kindles and the like that's it's hard to see how this trend will fade. If one electronic portable device can carry 1000 books then think of the storage savings. Imagine a library. The whole building could be held on one machine that someone can download unlimited copies to portable readers. It's also great news for new authors, launching a new author is hugely expensive, imagine the costs involved in printing thousands of books that no one buys. An e-download will be so much cheaper and less of a risk. It's great for readers as well. Your e-bookshelf can be scanned and new recommendations will be made based on your previous preferences. How nice would that be?

Physical books like handwriting are going to become elitist or subversive; they will leave the mainstream and peel away into cliques and collectible, underground fanatics and specialists. Rather like they used to be in the past, books will become things of beauty, bindings will become more extravagant and individual. In the middle ages books were bound in jewels, or shells as well as cloth or leather. Cloth was often embroidered and the leather was tooled to incredible intricacies. The art of book binding will soon be on the rise again and I for one welcome the idea of holding a hand stitched book bound in embroidered crewel work with hand tinted end papers.

But this is the 21st century and there are some new ideas floating around. Book art is a particularly charming one, where the whole book itself is a piece of work. I'm not sure how easy it would be to read but it sure is lovely to look at. I suspect Lewis Carroll would have loved to play around with book art, just think of a hole carved into the pages of a book where Alice falls down the rabbit hole and the text weaves across the blank pages. Of course it's not just authors playing with the book format; it's also publishers and artists. Penguin (again; they really are leading the pack in design innovation) recently released a range of classic titles with blank front covers for you to draw on, to make your own book. Rather flies in the face of your parents telling you not to scribble in your book.

Pop-up books are the first step in book art and who doesn't love pulling levers and tabs or having dinosaurs leap out at us in glorious 3D then opening envelopes and flaps to discover clues and hidden messages. There are even scratch and sniff books but a Fungus the Bogeyman scratch and sniff book is maybe a step too far!

So don't worry if the idea of new technology wiping out the book trade worries you. It won't happen, the industry will adapt and you'll get both the convenience of modern e-readers and the tactile joy of beautifully produced books. And I will set up reading rooms with leather armchairs where we can sip wine together surrounded by oak book cases laden with lovely, tactile, physical books!

Mevagissey Floods

It had been another windy and rainy night but at 6am a car drove past and suddenly it sounded like there had been an explosion. I looked out the window and a car was clearly struggling on the road. This was the first indication that something had happened overnight. I got up to see what had occurred and found a blown out manhole cover, the driver obviously hadn't seen it in the driving rain and flooded road and had gone straight into the hole.

I switched on the radio to see if the rain had affected anyone else to discover reports of landslides, helicopter rescues, front doors blown off, cars floating in roads and all this happening right on my doorstep. You listen to things like this in horror and fascination as you stand in your dry house wondering how it could be so bad just half a mile away in all directions.

Of course as the reports came in on Radio Cornwall I began to realize that whilst the house was dry, the warehouse was right in the middle of the affected area, at the bottom of a hill, by a river. Books and water just don't mix so Steve got in the car to see how close he could get and see if we still had a business. He had to park on the bypass and walk down to the warehouse and described a road that was a river and a lake where Cornish Market World sits. St Austell Bay Business Park though was dry. Whilst he was walking in I suddenly realized that Mevagissey where the shop is might also be in trouble. There was no mention of Meva on the radio but I called Mum and asked her what she could see. More bad news, Fore Street, Church Street and Market Square were underwater and the storm drain was like a cauldron. By a fluke of street levels Jetty Street was again dry.

So now I'm typing this thanking god for our good luck and hoping no one is hurt and that damaged property can be dealt with as quickly as possible. The children's school is inaccessible so I have two rather happy children here, one mine, one that I take in. Her father is trying to get his son to Truro as the railway line is closed due to landslides. Eldest son has gone into school but I imagine that it will be disrupted services there today as well.

Steve is now walking back for a fry up and we're keeping an eye on Mevagissey; the news reports that Mevagissey is completely closed off at the moment and Mum says the water levels are continuing to rise as the flood waters from St Austell flow down. High tide is at lunch but if it stays dry hopefully the worst of it will have drained away before then.

Two days have passed since I wrote that and now we can see how much damage has been caused. It's heartbreaking to hear of the losses but so wonderful to hear how everyone has pulled together. If we can help in anyway, please call in.

Meva is open, honest!

Well after a month of sunshine the rain has started which can only mean one thing, the Easter holidays are upon us. Whilst I'm sorry the rain has arrived I'm very glad that the holidays are here because it means that the season is back underway and here in Mevagissey it couldn't come soon enough.

Following the floods last December trade has been pretty dire. So many shops had to be gutted out that the place looked like a ghost town, people stayed away and when they returned there were closed shops all over the place and they left again. Understandable of course but for those of us who hadn't closed it's been grim, actually it's been grim for all of us but now that's all behind us. Like the daffodils happily waving in the breeze and the birds singing their hearts out, spring is here and Mevagissey is up and running.

In fact, as they say, it's an ill wind that blows no good. It's as though Meva has had a massive spring clean. Some businesses have changed hands, some have moved premises, others decided that that was enough and they've closed, making way for new ventures.

Brocante has expanded into the Holistic Mermaid so now there's even more gorgeous things to drool over. The Holistic Mermaid has moved into one of the empty galleries and will now be offering 15 minute holistic pick me ups in their treatment room. Expansion is clearly in the air because Portmellon Trading are opening up in Jason's old place. It's going to be called Issey, after our saint and will stock a line called Braintree – sort of like Seasalt. So now that's four great clothes shops we have in the village.

Curio Corner and Avellana look fabulous following their refit and we're spoilt for choice for a good place to sit down and have a coffee now that Market Square Cafe have re-opened to join Cofro, Bon Appetit and others offering great drinks and snacks. If you want something more substantial, Salamanda's and Alvorada's continue to receive great reviews for their evening menus.

Of course Mevagissey is more than just great shops and pubs, we have a fabulous museum and aquarium and the Mevagissey Model Railway celebrates its 40th birthday this year. Our harbour continues to thrive, nothing stops those fishermen, although our blackboard puzzles outside Hurley Books does make them pause for a second, then they work it out and wander off laughing at us for making them too easy, or cursing us for making them too tricky.

I know many of us arrive in Mevagissey by car but the walk from Portmellon or Pentewan along the coast path is wonderful, admittedly it is a bit up and down but at least it helps burn off the ice creams! Another great way to approach Meva is down the valley from Heligan, wandering down through the woods and fields is so relaxing, with only birdsong and streams to listen to and bluebells to look at. Well, I imagine it can be like that I normally have two noisy boys and one destructive dog but I like to think that serenity could be achieved on this walk. Probably the best way to arrive in Mevagissey though is the one that avoids all hills and that's by sea. I am aware that some people don't have their own private yacht but that's OK you can always use the Mevagissey to Fowey Ferry and try to spot basking sharks and dolphins joining you on your crossing.

However you do decide to come to Mevagissey I hope that when you get here you like all the changes and make the most of the village whilst we are all still relatively quiet.

See you soon.

Royalty and Radio

What do you know? Royalty must read my column! Do you remember the other week when I said that there were lots of great ways to visit Mevagissey but the best way was by boat? Well on Tuesday, HRH Sophie, Countess of Wessex came to visit Mevagissey to re-open the Tourist Information Centre and to see how businesses were managing after the floods and she came by boat! It was quite funny, she got dropped off at the lighthouse and was then driven down to the front of the harbour. It's hardly a big walk but I guess they have incredibly packed timetables so every second counts. It was nice to have someone come and have a look about and see what's what. It's great to see businesses up and trading again but more importantly there are still people who aren't back in their homes yet and I hope that they soon are.

HRH was then whisked onto Heligan, where she would have been assailed by wonderful scenery and glorious scents. It's lucky that she didn't come into St Austell then, poor thing would have been assailed by an altogether less fragrant smell. I have no idea where the smell is that is coming from but it smells like rotting cabbages. I'm sure I'm not the only person who went to

B&Q to get a set of drain rods, I know people are talking about it being connected to the brewery and the smell is definitely present on Trevarthian Road but I think people should investigate the DIY shops first, I bet they're doing a roaring trade in drain rods and cleaners!

Even if the Countess of Wessex had wanted to sample the fragrance for herself I wonder if she would have made it back out of the town. I have never known so many road works; the council seems to be acting as though it has a sum of money that it must spend before May is finished. It doesn't matter where I go I'm hitting bollards and traffic lights, some days I'm hitting three on one journey and they're like mushrooms, overnight they suddenly pop up and so the school run is taking longer and longer and getting more convoluted. Hey ho, if it means no more pot holes then I'm all for it. I do wonder though why it can't be done at night?

On a more positive note we are now the proud sponsors of a radio show. Hurley Books sponsor the Carclaze School show on Radio St Austell Bay on Tuesdays from 4pm – 5pm. 105.6 f.m. I know I'm biased but it's a great show, run by Janet and Simon, every week children come from the school and chat about, amongst other things, what they are reading. This week's book is Pip of Pengersick

"Adopted into a family of Cornish smugglers, Pip takes to life on the high seas. An encounter with a well-dressed stranger sends Pip and her smuggler friend. Harry, on a secret mission to France, a country in the grip of revolution. What is this secret that people will kill for? And who are the shadowy figures that dog their every footstep?"

Sounds exciting doesn't it? It's aimed at eight to eleven year olds so if you know someone in that bracket maybe they would like to read along and see what the pupils at Carclaze make of it next week?

It's great to have a truly local radio station and it's also really nice to hear children on the radio, on a show aimed at children. I honestly can't think of another current radio show anywhere, locally or nationally that is just for children so well done RASB! Maybe the pupils of Poltair or Penrice would like to run a later show for teenagers?

What do we need more – wild spaces or homes?

Do you remember me saying a few months that if it's a black and white issue then I would see the grey? Well now I'm seeing Carn Grey and the proposed eco town. This area around Carn Grey and Baal pit is one of my favourite walks with Harry, I'm generally up there every other day and if you're wondering who I am, then I'm the one standing on my own shouting at the top of my voice "If you don't get back here, right NOW I'll turn your ears into mittens!!" Harry will be out of sight somewhere terrorising rabbits and being eternally grateful that his owner never calls him back. – Selective deafness has Harry.

We love this area because it provides so many permutations of walks and a huge sense of space and wilderness. I also love the range of habitats; moorland, heathland, woods, fields, ponds, industrial landscapes and granite outcrops. I love the bizarre turquoise lakes, from some points you can see various lakes all in different shades of blue and green, further adding to the alien landscape. I found out recently that old episodes of Doctor Who were filmed in Baal Pit which seems fitting because whenever I walk over some of the sections I feel like I'm on a Martian territory watching terraforming in process. So much money has been spent on stabilising the landscape and introducing species to start to knit together the clay waste and it's really working well.

It's an incredible process; first tiny mosses take hold, with the odd heather and rhodo self seeding, for once a welcome intruder; trees have been planted and whilst the wild deer up there have tried to have a few nibbles they have been mostly foiled by the tree guards. A couple of times these deers have sprung out at me and I'm usually more surprised than them as I was expecting a Harry, not a Bambi. It's always a thrill to be so close to such a large wild animal.

I know a lot of people see the china clay workings as a horrific scar on the landscape but it seems that the telescope of time has a softening effect, the tin mines are now romantic tourist attractions but I bet at the time they were also seen by many as ugly monstrosities.

I know I'm not the only one up here as I often meet other dog walkers and anglers, walkers, bikers, bird watchers and joggers and during the snows other tobogganists and snow boarders screaming with laughter down the perfect slopes. Throughout the summer shouts of fun drift up from the swimming ponds, and in a different area, cubs and scouts set fire to things because as Arkala says "that's what boys like to do"

So I find the idea of an eco-town tearing up this place something of an irony. Do we really need this massive development? I know we need homes that people can afford to buy and I'd want all new buildings to be as environmental as possible, but I've never been able to afford a true eco house. I'm not against building new homes and I'm all for them being as "eco" as possible above and beyond guidelines. But why here? I have fewer objections to the proposed development behind Poltair, the land is stable, and it's closer to town and amenities and is less of a wild space.

On being famous

I think it's fair to say that down here in Cornwall people don't seem to be that bothered by celebrity. Film and TV stars wander around and locals look at them briefly wondering where they recognise them from or give a nod and a hi and go on their way. The other day a group of us were on a dog walk and passed Dawn French, we all nodded and smiled, as you do when you pass someone on a footpath, and continued on. No great shakes, no gushing, no autographs, we just get on with it and we let people get on with their lives as well. I've often heard singers and the like who live in Cornwall giving interviews on the radio saying that living in Cornwall is great because everyone treats them just like anyone else. A while back my brother met Andrew Ridgley at a dinner party; did they talk about Wham, the fame, the fortune? Nope, they discussed their golfing handicaps and pudding.

So all these recent stories concerning Jimmy Saville has made me think about the way people behave towards famous people. Whilst he hasn't been convicted of anything it does appear that over the decades there have been numerous complaints against him that were ignored, hushed up or just not believed. Can you imagine how scary and humiliating the world must have seemed to these young girls? To have such terrible things happen to them but then to not be believed either? It really does beggar belief. Was he so well respected that no one would believe it or was there a culture of cover up going on or was the money he raised in fund raising really worth turning a blind eye for? I find the whole affair hard to understand. I always thought he was an unpleasant character and when he died I heard comments from some along the lines of "let's see what will come out of the woodwork now" but I couldn't believe anything would. Just because someone seems creepy doesn't mean that they are, and surely, surely no one could get away with so much when they were so frequently in the public eye?

In the same week Lance Armstrong has been found guilty of illegal drug use. He denies the claims but won't contest them and now a whole host of people have come forward to say his cheating was constant over the years. Again, the only way for him to get away with it was with massive support from his team members. It seems so harsh that a man who survived cancer and went on to win massively will now only be remembered as a drugs cheat.

I just think the UK media needs to take a look at how Cornwall does things and follow suit. Treat people at face value, don't allow them to get away with stuff just because they are famous, and say well done only when something is well done.

Back to the boot camp

Well I said I'd let you know how I'm doing at Boot Camp and I have to say that I'm still alive and so are my family and I'm lighter and slimmer but it hasn't been easy. This is my diary.

End of Week One and I could only praise the powers that be that not only am I still alive but so too is my family. Giving up coffee was not funny. As an early riser the morning starts haven't been too horrific, not good but not "kill me now", that was reserved for the food plan. In all fairness the food sheet is very sensible, lots of fish, meat, fruits, vegetables, nuts and water all very balanced, all very sensible but really who enjoys sensible? The idea was that on my non-contact days with Petra I would do more exercise on my own via some sheets and videos that she has sent out. I have to be honest I haven't done them yet. Day one and two I was too tired from getting up at a silly time, day three and four my head really hurt by day five and six my energy levels were failing and my kidneys hurt and I was hugely fed up. Every time Petra asked for a smile all she got was a grimace with bared teeth.

End of Week Two. This week I've woken up feeling better, no headache no aching kidneys, finally drinking enough water. Can't stand the stuff but my previous liquid intake was provided by alcohol and caffeine. So I will do the interim exercises next week and hopefully see more benefits, so far lost 5 lbs and inches all over the place. I know that next week is unlikely to be so spectacular but a loss is a loss. Some really cold mornings. Exercising whilst listening to owls is weird.

End of Week Three. More width and weight loss which made me feel a bit sparkier.

Unfortunately it was half term so still no additional workouts. Also found it harder to stick to the diet sheet when the boys and their friends were around and there were loads of treats lying about. God help me at Christmas as I have no willpower. Feeling bright all week and finding the early mornings easy. Width loss but no weight loss.

Start of Week Four. As I write this I'm in my final week so I won't be able to give you final figures but the blog will have the final measurements. I'm now feeling brighter and have started on the additional workouts (they're awful - mad woman keeps saying "Isn't this fun!" You can almost see her exclamation marks). The clocks going back have also meant fewer exercises by moonlight and owl calls.

So after three weeks where am I? Well I've lost 7.5 lbs and between three and four inches at all vital points, that's a loss of 26.5 inches overall so far. So in terms of weight loss it's not dramatic, in terms of a better figure and a healthier body then I'm pleased with it.

Will I do this next month? You bet! This has been a really enjoyable way to get ready for all the Christmas parties. The crowd I train with are incredible friendly and supportive, men and women of all ages, sizes and fitness levels. I haven't met the evening team but I bet they're just as nice. Petra doesn't let you slack and at your private weekly measurement sessions she's really supportive. There's also loads of great recipes on her website. Although let's be honest there's only so much that you can do with pumpkin. I am still seriously missing the coffee though!

The London Book Fair

This has been a really frantic week for us as we went up to the London Book Fair. This fair is the most important event in the publishers' calendar and gives the world a chance to buy and sell rights for new titles, announce new authors, launch new products and generally get together and put the world to rights (or not, depending on how gloomy looking forward makes you – and to be fair, booksellers do tend to be a backward looking lot).

We figured that the best way to prepare for four days in London would be to spend the Sunday on the beach and catching as many waves as we could. With our salt glands fully loaded we caught the sleeper and woke up to noise, dirt and heat. The Book Fair was fascinating and it was great to get a glimpse at the new releases, meet some authors and listen to the industry warnings about e-books. Boy, were there a lot of warnings and it's probably fair to say looking at the American trend, that within five years maybe 50% of fiction sales will be downloads rather than hard copy books. A truly alarming figure for those running bookshops but rather than harping back to the good old days (whenever they were) I think those that will weather the change will be those businesses that find a niche or a new angle and to be honest 'twas ever thus!

As much as I enjoyed the Fair I also enjoyed exploring areas of London that I didn't know. I've never lived in London so have never really had time to explore but this time we got some chances to escape. My first treasure was Brompton Cemetery, it was a beautiful place and whilst nowhere in London is really quiet it was very calm, full of tame ravens and squirrels and Victorian statues, crypts and overgrown tombstones. I used to love doing my revision in Norwich graveyard and found that this cemetery provided the same calming influence.

I then went on to explore the Inns of the Court of London, another oasis of peace and calm, beautiful gardens and stunning architecture laid out in academic quadrants connected by little alleys and hidden between the Thames, Fleet Street and the City of London proper. It was lovely to sit under a magnolia tree not yet in bloom watching a barrister dash past in wig and gown listening to a fountain behind me. It doesn't beat Cornwall but it beat being stuck in Starbucks at Piccadilly Circus by a country mile.

I also discovered two mad museums both fronting onto Lincoln's Inn Fields. The John Soane's Museum is the home of a Victorian collector who filled his house with all and everything that he found on his travels. The place is full of pediments, Doric columns, Egyptian burial chambers, writing tables, vases, paintings and so on. It's a full to the brim, hotch-potch of stuff. Almost directly opposite it, across the square, is the Hunterian Museum of the Royal College of Surgeons. Again, full to the brim of oddities but what oddities! The place is full of skeletons and pickling jars of human and animal bits and pieces. Many of the times the things I was looking at were mesmerising and beautiful but then I would look to the next item and recoil as I found myself eyeballing a rabbit foetus. There really were some truly bizarre exhibits, human skulls showing defects, or nervous systems removed and pinned out on wooden boards. Eventually I escaped into the Library, a place of leather armchairs and leather binding with the hushed, hallowed silence of a room that was not concerned for its future, knowing that its role was forever secured.

Maybe, I too am someone who loves to look backwards.

What I did on my weekend

I've had a great weekend but it became obvious to me that it's been a while since I've been out to play. I'm exhausted now and wondering if maybe age is more than just a state of mind. I got my first reminder of how long I've been out of circulation when I went to buy Steve and I a drink and the total came to £6 something. I say six pounds something because quite frankly when the barman said "six" my brain went into paralysis and a weird buzzing noise filled my ears, with a sort of dumb shock I handed over my £10 note and left with change that did indeed only include three shiny coins plus shrapnel. Sitting down with Steve I studied my small glass of wine, I deliberately chose the small option in case it wasn't nice and at Steve's pint of Doom Bar, with a certain amount of awe. We were in a nice country pub (I won't name names) but it wasn't somewhere where I expected city prices. In fact I had better not go to a city pub now without my cards, cash probably won't be enough.

We were gradually joined by other friends who had all come out for a friend's birthday party. It was great to see so many of us in a pub, in the evening, with no children, that in itself was a celebration and we all made the most of it. We also met some new people who were great company; it's always such fun to discover new conversations and ways of looking at the world. A loud and happy evening eventually came to an end, to be naturally followed by a delicate morning. Of course in the past I would spend such mornings being quiet and gentle, no sudden movements and the only strenuous exercise being to switch the kettle on. But not now. Not now that my boys play rugby and I have a dog that needs a walk. So dodging showers, and it really lashed it down this morning, we got Harry walked, the children suited and booted and made it to Truro – (it would be an away match) with only minutes to spare. The ground was very soft, in fact the lower field had clover and reeds growing in it – not good signs! Our U12s were beaten by, I'm afraid to say, a very good team, but if you're going to be beaten at least let it be by the best. Our U10s however won their match as convincingly as the U12s lost theirs so balance was restored and as both of my boys scored a try there was peace on the drive home.

Of course returning home still meant no rest for us as it's back to school tomorrow so uniforms to be ironed kit to be scrapped down then washed, bags to be packed, homework to be checked, projects finished off, all done at full volume. And in the middle of all this I'm trying to finish off my VAT return. Well I've done it now or else I wouldn't be typing this. So a nice hectic weekend to round off an enjoyable half term, I hope everyone had as good a weekend.

Mothering Sunday

So, Mothering Sunday is almost upon us. Traditionally it falls on the 4th Sunday in lent, which this year is on the 18th of March. This Christian festival, which dates back to roman times when it was used to honour the Virgin Mary, is a celebration of motherhood. In later years it became a day for servants to enjoy with their families at a time when the working week was far longer than it is now but, as time went on, the custom began to peter out. Mothering Sunday enjoyed a revival in the 1920's when a lady named Constance Penswick Smith created the mothering Sunday movement. The revival gathered pace during the second world war as American soldiers serving overseas began to observe the traditions of mothering Sunday and it wasn't very long before some bright spark saw the commercial potential. Heavily promoted, Mothering Sunday, or mother's day, became the dream date for every florist and card manufacturer up and down the country.

And so we arrive at the present day. I have two children and I also have a husband who is less than enthusiastic about observing the traditions of this auspicious day. Steve has always felt that he must make the effort, particularly where the boys are concerned. When they were younger they were plonked at the dining room table with crayons and blank paper and told to "make a nice card for mummy". These creations were, of course, lovely and I still have most of them somewhere. As they have grown older Steve has taken them into town, given them a fiver each, and pointed them in the direction of Poundland. Young children always work on the basis that five presents are better than one. Steve works on the premise that the boys are choosing the presents so they must be special. Some of the more memorable gifts over the years include a bag of bird seed, a spatula and some rubber gloves. There has also been a lot of chocolate, some of which I've eaten.

This year could be interesting because the boys now get pocket money and Steve, being an ex-financial adviser, is determined that they learn to budget. So, whatever I get this year, will be after their weekly spend on phone top ups, sweets and magazines. I'm not hopeful but, then, I don't mind because whatever they get me will be wonderful. Although their best presents have always be the ones they made themselves. Incidentally, I don't wish to give the impression that my husband stints on his own mothers gift. His parents live in Blandford, Dorset, and there is no Poundland there so he sends his mum flowers every year. I love flowers and am considering a move to Blandford myself.

Almost 13 years ago my eldest son was born on mothering Sunday. As I was lying in the hospital bed coming to terms with motherhood the midwife came in and asked what I was getting for mother's day. I replied that having just given birth and having been in labour for, what felt like, days, It was the last thing on my mind and that, anyway, my mum would understand. The midwife gave a nod towards the baby by my side and said "I wasn't talking about your Mum, I was talking about you!" That was the very moment when I realised my world had changed completely.

I hope all you Mothers out there have a wonderful day.

We honestly can't do it without you

So that's the spring term over. It's always funny in the car park on the last day of term when the school secretary wishes me a good holiday. Holiday! With the children home, a business to run and the season underway? Her grin always seems to be bordering on the evil side as she drives away to three weeks without the constant clamour of a hundred little voices. It's fair to say though, that my grin is equally evil at the start of term when I drop the children off and get back to my work or "my holiday" as I like to think of term time.

With the onset of Easter it also means that the rugby season is finally coming to an end. This was the boys' first season as I had stuck my heels in for years. My children were far too precious to come home looking like Gordian knots, broken and bleeding and covered in mud. Mostly everyone looked on at me in amazement, what precious children? Those two boys that spent most of their lives throwing themselves off piers, climbing up trees, fighting each other at the drop of a hat and competing about anything and generally covered in blood, bruises and mud? Were those the two precious angels that mummy wanted to protect? Well, there's nowt so blind as a mother's love and I finally relented to years of pressure and let them go. My mistake? Not to have let them go sooner! They have had a fabulous time, made new friends and have learnt great discipline and team skills. They have two wonderful coaches, Paul and Richard amongst others that helped them settle in, played to their strengths and worked on their weaknesses. At the beginning my eldest was a bit concerned about the mauls (well who could blame him?) he would run forward and then as he got to about a meter from the maul he would hit an invisible force field that seemed to repel him. He would bounce around on the edges, hopping forward, jumping back every time the throng of arms and legs seemed to get too close. Obviously working on a kill or cure ethos, Richard made him a second row and now he's there in the thick of it.

Lankelly Fowey is a great little club and always has room for more children, they train on Saturday mornings and play matches on Sunday mornings and have a lovely attitude toward rugby.

Of course I won't get my weekends back because as soon as the rugby ends the windsurfing and sailing starts up. We do this over at Polkerris, who have really set up a great water sports school in a very short space of time. Bob and Ann have performed miracles over the last three years and have even won awards for their efforts. Again, here are more people that love what they do and really want to pass on their enthusiasm to anyone that will listen.

If there's a point to this rambling column I suppose it's twofold; the first is that there are always things for kids to do, scouts and guides, team sports, par athletics track, sailing and so on. The second is that these things are available because there are people out there that give up their time just to help, support and encourage. Some do it because it's their business, others because it's their job and others because it's their passion. So thanks to all of you. Not just because it's brilliant to have my children taken off my hands (although that's fairly major) but also because you're helping to give my children and other children, a really great childhood.

Digging up St Austell

We are often asked if we plan to re-open another shop in St. Austell and every time my heart and head are torn. We left St Austell five years ago as our lease had expired; we tried desperately to find another property but found the rents to be exorbitant and were often found to be cheaper in Truro. Looking around we couldn't see what justified the high fees. Trade was depressed, the main high street was being constantly ripped up, a new development was apparently due to be built but that seemed to be pie in the sky. Eden had been up and running for a few years, to dramatic success but no one seemed to be coming into St Austell. Over one million people a year within five miles of my shop but I wouldn't have known it. St Austell, Cornwall's largest population centre, no restaurant, few shops and the cinema about to close down. No I couldn't understand the high leases at all.

We moved to Charlestown, into the tiny weighbridge and discovered something amazing. We made more money in that tiny cabin, in a tiny village than we did in St Austell and that was taking one full trading year as comparison. What on earth was going on? Well our regular customers stuck with us but we suddenly gained the visitors. Right under our noses were lots of people looking to buy books in pleasant surroundings. Now we're in Mevagissey and loving it but I still look at St Austell and wonder what in the name of God is happening.

The new development is up and running and there is a lovely vibrancy beginning, regeneration plans are underway and I love the china clay walks, the museum, the Carnival but despite all the incredible hard work by the residents and traders, St Austell is still being trashed. The high street is a total shambles, you can barely see the shops let alone get to them and now the council wants to put up the parking charges. I could weep and I imagine that quite a few traders already are.

St Austell is such an obvious focal point. We have a main line train station, within seven miles of us we have Eden, an international attraction, a world heritage site in Luxylyan and Charlestown, Britain's favourite garden (Heligan), miles of beaches, cycle tracks, woods; why are people who stay near Fowey or Mevagissey not spending a day or evening in St Austell? Why do locals shop in Truro?

So will we open in St. Austell? Regretfully no, not yet because as much as I want to support St Austell I don't want to go bankrupt doing it. When I can see that St Austell is finally being used as the hub that it should be for locals and visitors alike then of course we'll want to be there and so will lots of other shops and restaurants. I suspect though that many town centres, not just St Austell, are all facing tough decisions about how they should be structured in the future. Our council just seems to be making things harder for us than is necessary.

Pottering on through life

This week is not going according to plan. It's not my sons' fault but I'm going to blame them anyway. Easter holidays have coincided with me working back in the shop again as we move back into full time opening and so I'm trying to write my articles, file my VAT returns, do the housework and run the shop all whilst trying to juggle the demands of the children. It's getting so much easier now that they are getting older but they still have no concept of the fact that just because they're on holiday doesn't mean that I'm on holiday.

I discovered the other day that there isn't a lower age limit for leaving your children unattended. You may not leave them in harm but that's it. I nearly booked a weekend away with Steve there and then. All those years when I could have left them but then that's the point isn't it? I don't need a law to tell me how to look after my children I already knew when they were too young and now, how much they can be trusted. Even so I can't bring myself to leave them for more than an hour but at least it means I can run errands without having to drag them along.

Harry gets dragged along, not that he minds because it means that there's a chance we'll stop somewhere for a walk. He is such a daft mutt, he greets everything with total enthusiasm and we're debating at the moment getting a second dog. He has been such a treasure that a second dog wouldn't be too much of a burden, the trouble is that dogs are so expensive. I'd like another puppy simply because we can all get used to each other, we have two cats, a dog, loud boys and busy lives and I'd hate an older dog to not be able to settle into our routine. We did go to the RSPCA shelters to investigate a rescue dog but it just didn't work out. Despite having a dog, our house would have to be checked which affronted Steve a bit but I suppose they need to cross the "t"s and dot the "i"s. Then we couldn't have some dogs because of the cats, other dogs because of Harry and finally most of the remaining dogs were ruled out because of the children. In the end only one dog was available, a four year old half mastiff! He was a sweetie but huge. It was all a bit disheartening really. What I want is another Springer or a Cocker; they're a lovely breed and in   theory will enjoy all the exercise that Harry already gets.

We shall have to keep our ears open and then maybe Harry will have someone to play with on our walks and when we go away he'll have company in the kennels. It will also make a nice change for him to have an animal at home that doesn't attack him whenever he goes up to say hello. The cats aren't normally vicious creatures but at 16 years old they draw the line at having something loud and hairy sniffing their bottoms. Can't say I blame them!

Fishermen

Like most shops the nation over we have a counter and on that counter we have a charity box and like most counters we only have space for one. For us it was an easy choice, the RNLI. We work in a coastal village; we play by and in the water all year long. I dive and if ever I was to get into trouble it would be the RNLI who would be first on the scene to summon a helicopter and get me to safety. More importantly my sister is a crewman over in Pembrokeshire. When things go pear shaped Anna and other unpaid volunteers like her run out into usually horrible weather and put themselves at risk to save others. Anna would very modestly point out that she generally just ends up towing back windsurfers who've ended up heading for America.

So for us it's the RNLI but if we had the space for a second box what would we have? I like Shelter Box enormously, I think what they do is great and simple so they would have initially been my second choice but a while back one of the fishermen asked why I didn't have a box out for the Fisherman's Mission. Now I have to be honest and say that I'd never heard of them, it conjured up Methodist choirs standing in draughty halls sucking revolting pastilles, but Jimmy had nothing but praise for them so I investigated a bit further.

Over 13,000 men and women work in the UK's toughest and most dangerous peacetime occupation: deep sea fishing. At sea, they face death and injury on a daily basis. On land, many face insecurity and debt. And life for the 50,000 retired fishermen and their dependants is no better, with debt, inadequate pensions and scant savings meaning no respite from hardship once the fishing's over.*

The Fisherman's Mission provides emergency aid when tragedy strikes and looks after injured fishermen or grieving families. They offer financial, practical and emotional support. They look after retired fishermen and fight their cases in tenancy disputes, ensure their homes are safe and that they are coping.

Fishing is one of the three traditional Cornish industries along with farming and mining. Well the miners have pretty much gone now and the farmers continue to struggle but the fishermen remain in a perilous industry unaltered in generations. I wonder how many of them have private health care, company pension schemes, how easy is it to go to a bank and raise a mortgage if your pay packet depends on winds and currents and sheer good luck? When I see the fisherman on the jetty mending their nets and shouting back and forth, laughing and joking I'm just glad that there is a charity that steps in and helps when times get tough. Maybe I will have to make room for a second box. * www.fishermensmission.org.uk

This week I've been reading The White Queen by Philippa Gregory, not impressed; drinking very bland wines, even less impressed and been listening to Tik Tok by Kesha as the boys love it. I've now heard it about a million times. Unimpressed all round really.

Are we really getting ruder?

The other day a gentleman came into the shop and raised his cap to me. It was a really nice moment and made me wish that hat wearing wasn't in decline; it's such a nice gesture. I, of course, nodded my head back, in fact more or less everyone who comes in the shop gets a nod, a smile of a "hello" and more or less everyone responds. It also doesn't matter which member of staff is on, they are all friendly and greet all our customers. It's not as though I even have to tell them, it's as natural to them as it is to me. So it came as a bit of a surprise to read that in a recent poll, that said Britons' were no ruder than they were 20 years ago, that the vast majority of people disagreed with the poll's findings. Apparently we think we're getting ruder. I do think we are getting more familiar. Nowadays it's kisses all round when friends meet up and I have to confess to wishing we were a little less Continental in this regard. What's wrong with a good handshake or a nod of the head, all this kissing and hugging is a bit much, but no harm is meant by it so I'll learn to live with it. But extra kissing isn't rudeness, well it might be a bit offensive if you don't know them but really it's not generally considered offensive.

And of course it's not just hugs and kisses where we've got more familiar, there's more of a breakdown between age gaps, children aren't silent until spoken too, men and women mix in pubs and terraces far more. All over society we mix in ways that we never used to which can sometimes lead to confusions and minor embarrassments but I still don't see that as rude. If a child interrupts me when I'm speaking I'll let them know that that they have to wait. I don't necessarily think the child is being rude, they're just learning. If the parent allows the child to interrupt then I think it is the parent that is being rude.

But I don't see rudeness as an issue of the younger generation any more than it is of the older one. I've lost count of the times when my boys and I go single file for an elderly pair of women – and I'm afraid it's always women – and they don't say thank you or smile or do anything. I don't expect them to go single file, they're older and slower but they are not blind or dumb. I should imagine that it is this sort of person that complains the loudest about rudeness in others.

I heard a nice story once about a man who was mending a hedge beside a road. A stranger came up to him and asked what the people in the next village were like. The labourer asked if he had been to the previous village down the road and when the man said he had, the labourer asked what he made of them there. "Oh they were among the nicest people I've ever met" said the stranger. "Ah well, you'll find the people in the next village just as friendly." A week later another stranger passed the labourer and asked the same question. Again the labourer asked the stranger what he thought of the people in the previous village. "Well they were awful, a bunch of thieves and villains." "Hmm," said the labourer, "in that case I'd avoid the next village if I were you."

Where ever you go, you always take you with you.

Going forward whilst in reverse

I've been going backwards a lot this week. Poor Harry, there he was shuffling and snuffling back and forth on one side of a wire fence that neither of us could see, hidden by brambles and bracken as it was, but nevertheless it was an invincible barrier. I tried to tell Harry that he needed to go back the way he came, re-join the path and come the long way around. Now anyone who thinks that a Springer Spaniel is capable of that level of reasoning is clearly less well endowed with creative logic than that Springer in question. In fact the idea that I had even tried to suggest it to Harry showed that neither of us were going to advance the evolutionary process very much in either of our respective kingdoms. So it was me not Harry that turned back and trudged along the path until I could re-join a by now whimpering, confused, fed up, dippy dog.

On another occasion I had stopped outside of the Grampound Smokehouse for some gorgeous prawn sarnies. I got back in my car reversed a bit to get a better angle out onto the road because sometimes it can be really tricky to join the traffic and then waited. Only a few moments had passed when someone flashed their lights at me. Immediately I accelerated but   backwards, I was still in reverse! Only the briefest of heartbeats later I selected the correct gear and this time accelerated forwards and on my way, blushing wildly.

Going backwards just seems wrong. I was listening to a chap from Google saying that it was a Google mantra to keep going forward at any cost. If you see a wall, climb over it. If there's a river on the other side, swim through it. If there are crocodiles, throw them your left arm and swim on. Nothing will stop you! Eeek. I don't know but isn't that all a bit extreme. What about find a boat? See if there's a bridge? Change your mind and go back? Maybe it's because for us time is a linear thing. We are always moving forward through time, although the seasons seem to be circular, August once again, but this August doesn't feel as warm as the last one, maybe it was a bit shorter, less got done. Maybe because we know we'll never be 21 again, it clouds everything we do, because we are driven towards the grave by our biology we feel determined to drive forwards in every other sphere of our lives. Maybe that's why the final space shuttle flight feels wrong. We are going backwards in terms of space exploration. Surely the final frontier was further than the moon for mankind?

But going backwards isn't always a mistake. I feel so proud of people who are able to say "No" or "Stop – this isn't working." To have the guts to say, "I've failed but I'm not going to keep failing. I hate this and I'm not going to do it anymore. You've promoted me a step too far I want to go back. I hate this university, I'm coming home. We're not good together I want to be single again."

Oh well I shall drift onwards, a little body in this massive universe all heading towards entropy and hopefully from time to time I'll remember to go backwards a bit. If I have Harry with me I will have no option but to go back regularly to retrieve him from various cul-de-sacs and maybe I'll see that as a good thing too.

Hello Agatha

Obviously I felt that I wasn't busy enough because this week I brought home a new puppy! We had always planned for Harry to have a companion and we thought he was now a good age to introduce a puppy, so whilst I was at the trainer's last week she mentioned a litter she knew of from a really reputable source. Off I went to have a look and of course you just can't look at puppies, so Agatha jumped into my arms and away we went.

So far she is a very clever little girl but she does require a plug. I forgot that after Harry I swore I wouldn't get a dog under six months. Hey ho, piddle and poo. Harry is treating the whole situation with a little jealousy and a lot of resignation. Hence the main reason for the gun dog training. We'll never go on a shoot but it gives him something new to learn and he gets to spend more time with me. I always think distraction is a great way of heading off problems before they develop.

As if taking on a puppy and new dog lessons wasn't enough exercise for me I have also started a new class with Petra called Boxercise, I swear I have never had so much fun! I wasn't sure what it was going to entail but I wandered along to the class and was a bit surprised to see pads and gloves. Hmm, not shadow boxing then. We spent a good half hour warming up, we then had to pay attention to a lot of safety rules and then we laced up our gloves and started to lay into our partners' pads. I partnered up with Kate and was the first to don the gloves. Poor Kate, she kept grinning at me every time I apologised and telling me to hit her harder. Strange girl but I soon got into the swing of it. No pun intended. We then swapped over and she laid into me. I tell you there is something really funny about laughing with someone whilst they try to punch you. Thankfully we never once made contact with each other, other than on the sparring pads but we both ended the session agreeing that gum shields might be an idea. Petra kept shouting at us to guard our faces and of course we were never aiming for the face but it only takes one tired accident before you see stars. I'm sure this won't happen but there was a lot of nervous giggling. Kate also came with her husband so they can carry on with their training behind the scenes. My money's on Kate.

Aside from that it's been the usual week of driving to work with the sea filing the horizon and listening to Radio 2 traffic reports of tailbacks and congestion across the nation's motorways whilst I slow down for rabbits and pheasants. Not a bad life all in all. Hope you all have a great weekend, I'll be playing taxi for a dinner party in Wadebridge, a rugby game in Bude, a sleepover in Lostwithiel and an outdoor activity day in Minions.

Those bunnies and birds better not get in my way as I'm going to be very busy!

Niggles and nibbles

Half term has passed us by and we all noticed that the roads seemed a bit busier than usual, Tescos was running out of stock faster than usual, on Saturday the queues at the petrol pumps were silly and gradually the county felt that little bit fuller. Now it's emptied out again but we all know that Easter is just around the corner and along with the visitors comes the good weather (well sometimes) the outdoor concerts, the plays in the park, the festivals, the events and shows which we all love. So even if I have to reverse 500 yards uphill every other day and never find anywhere to park I still love the start of spring and everything and everyone else that comes with it.

At the moment I'm supposed to be concentrating on writing this column but life seems to have jumped into a handcart and is on its way to hell. The chief issue is the printer that seems convinced that the A4 paper that is in the tray is not actually A4. Its way of drawing our attention to the problem is by printing the same packing slip every time with an accompanying note saying that this isn't A4, so clearly there's a fault but it has nothing to do with the size of the paper. Now we can't print any of our customers' orders and the backlog is building. Typically I am at home and Steve is in the warehouse trying to fix it and trying to flag down the nearest saint so that he may steal their patience because I'm afraid I've worn out all of his. It's hard to know who finds the following sentence more frustrating, "have you wiggled the blue toggle?" I'm exasperated because wiggling the blue toggle would be the first blatantly obvious thing to do. Steve is exasperated because he doesn't know what a blue toggle is, where to find it or how to wiggle it. In a minute I'll have to drive back to the warehouse, which I don't want to do because I've just left there and returned home to find the puppy has been sick everywhere, won't eat her food and is looking pretty fed up with life. I have just cleaned up the wee, poo and sick and I too, am looking pretty fed up with life.

I was going to write about cookery programmes as they are a nice way for me to switch off and think of new ways of serving some of my favourites. Clarissa Dickson-Wright made me laugh the other night, on the boning of rabbits; she suggested that you could ask your local butcher to do but "really, don't be so wet!" and on the whole squeamishness about eating bunnies? "Don't be so ridiculous" It was like having one's Nanny come and put you straight. Nigel Slater is another favourite for putting together some great tastes but does he have to be so earnest in his delivery? He sounds like he's addressing NATO and Lex Luther has the bomb! It's only anchovies Nigel, breathe deeply. His current series is all about making leftovers last to another meal.

Yesterday he cooked a family pie and showed us how to make a lunch out of it the following day. Now clearly Nigel isn't cooking for a family because the clue is in the title "family pie". When I cook a family pie it feeds the family, there are no leftovers. Ho hum, the other clue that Nigel isn't cooking for a family is his ridiculously clean fridge, devoid of any form of junk or basic staples. Just the odd parcel of meat lovingly wrapped in brown paper. Well, he doesn't live in my world but sometimes I wished I lived in his.

On well back to my life, sorry I've not been on form today but it's all been a bit of a mess. Hope you're all getting along fine and enjoying a quick break from your daily chores, whatever they may be.

Goodbye 205

Well it's been a sad week for me as my unreliable little car has finally gone to ground. I knew things were beginning to get a bit dire when along with not being able to hold a charge in the battery it started to drip oil and guzzle water. These failings became quite clear at the Royal Cornwall Show. We set off late on Saturday, just before lunch and took our normal route via Burlawn, however we had never travelled so late before and I found myself stuck in the tiny lanes in a stationery queue of traffic. It seemed that the lower car parks had filled up and so we were having to travel past the showground over the A39 and into the top fields. It seemed daft for us all to be sat in traffic so Steve and the boys hopped out and walked the few hundred yards up to the entrance. As I sat there I noticed that the temperature gauge seemed to be climbing, now I'd topped up the radiator before I left so I wasn't too concerned, 10 minutes later though, having only moved a few metres the gauge was heading towards red and I was now getting alarmed. The lane I was sat in was one car wide; if I broke down I would be the most unpopular person in all of Cornwall. So I decided we weren't going anywhere quickly and turned the engine off to give the radiator a chance to cool down. A few minutes later and the traffic started to move again. I turned the key and heard the horrifying sound of my car feebly attempting to turn the engine over and then giving up. In the field next to me a couple were eating their lunch in the camp site; we looked at each other in horror and then looked back down the line of traffic. I can only say that what she mouthed to me pretty much mirrored what I had just said to myself. Incredibly, where the car had broken down there was a tiny widening of the road, enough for me to be pushed out of the way. Embarrassed I got out asking for help from the car behind me and it was one of those lovely moments when out jumped three blokes from their 4X4. They pushed the car to one side and then gave the battery a jump! Grateful, I struggled on, and by the time I got to the top car park the radiator was in the red and all the warning lights were on and flashing "STOP".

From here on the car was on borrowed time. Did I go to the expense of replacing the battery and fixing the oil and water leak? I couldn't help but feel we had passed the point of diminishing returns. Then one morning on the drive to school something gave a large metallic twang from underneath, the car jolted and shuddered a bit and then drove on normally. It did it three more times on the drive home and I was a nervous wreck by the time I had parked up. At 20 years old and with over 2000000 miles on the clock I figured that it had probably come to the end of its life. Despite the car's recent issues it has been a terrific powerhouse. It's had to endure Harry moulting everywhere, fish defrosting in the footwell, pheasants bleeding in the boot and more sand than can be found on Par beach. It stank, was permanently dirty and looked dreadful, the body work looked as though someone had taken a blow torch to it and stripped off all the paint. Probably for all the wrong reasons I was always recognized out on the road, no

82

other car could quite match my 205 for sheer awfulness. But it kept on going and cost very little to run and I was always very protective of my decaying little heap. Soon I will have something shiny, neither fish nor foul will be allowed to decompose, Harry will be banished to the boot and the boys will clean their feet before getting in. I'll miss the old car but it will be nice to get in a car that doesn't smell like an abattoir in summer and doesn't break down at the drop of a hat.

And Goodbye Mr B

Once again, the school holidays are upon us. Our youngest son, who is still at primary school, broke up on Friday. He, of course, is overjoyed, much to the annoyance of our oldest son, who is at secondary school and does not break up for a few more weeks. This has caused much disgruntlement in the Hurley household and the cry of "it's not fair" is regularly heard over the morning porridge. My husband, sympathy personified, fires back his standard witty response "life's not fair" and gives his "best years of your life…" speech. Mostly to deaf ears though.

The youngest boy's school really goes to town on the last day of the summer term. Parents, grandparents, ex-pupils, Governors, ex-teachers and Uncle Tom Cobley and all cram into the school hall for the final assembly and the highlight of the school year, prize giving. It's a time when sporting prowess and academic achievement are recognised and applauded. And, bearing in mind that it is a primary school, there are cups for things like best handwriting, politeness and most improved footballer. Each winner is called out and goes up to the stage where he or she shakes hands with the headmaster and collects the cup from the visiting dignitary whilst the audience clap and cheer. Proud mothers often wipe a tear away before the mascara gets smudged and fathers swallow the lump in their throat as their beaming progeny collect their treasured prize.

This year our lad won a cup for scoring the most rounders in the inter house rounders competition. In previous years he has walked away with the golf, football, tennis, cross country and swimming cups. Much to my disappointment the trophy cabinet has not been overly bothered by any academic awards. His father is very proud though but, as the ultimate competitive dad, feels that Finn has been "robbed" of some of the cups. When some of the children's names were announced I thought he was going to demand a stewards' enquiry.

Leavers assembly this year was especially poignant as the headmaster, Mr Bradley, is moving on to another post in Oman after 11 years as head and one of the most popular teachers is retiring. Also, the caretaker has decided to hang up his hammer and the head cook her whisk, as they both head off to retirement. The assembly was as much a celebration of them as it was for the children, and we all wish them the best of luck for the future. A new head starts next year and we will see how she stamps her mark on the life of the school.

In the meantime I have weeks looming ahead of me, trying to juggle work and bored children. At least being self-employed means a greater degree of flexibility than many, the problem is that if I don't do my work no one else will and I won't get paid. I can see some late nights ahead as the candle gradually burns away at both ends. Just as it nears the end of its wick and I, the end of my patience, the summer holidays will once more be a thing of the past and a new chapter will begin at our junior school.

Green Foundations

I've just started on a course run by the Green Foundation at Eden. It's run over a few weeks and is aimed at local businesses in an effort to make them more aware of climate issues and sustainability. It was quite a change to go back into a more formal business environment and reminded me why I was quite glad to leave it all behind me in the first place. I'm not good with strangers and quite happy to disagree with people so not the best start. In fact when I went into the room two tables were filling up with people chatting to each other and getting to know one and other. I went and sat on the empty table. Gradually my table also began to fill up but funnily enough, it began to fill up with other people who were quite happy to keep their own company. One quiet, polite table, two bubbly tables. I think the course organisers must have looked at us with concern. Embarrassment inducing "get to know you" exercises continued and more and more people got into the spirit of things. My table seemed to retreat into itself but we were beginning to share a few raised eyebrows and grimaces with each other. Progress of a sort. Gradually and at our own speed we got to know each other and soon we were as likely to be told off for talking as any other table.

Eden makes for such a wonderful venue to host a course, we were often wandering off into the gardens either to discuss things or just have a coffee. Lectures were varied and interesting and the team work – yes I cringed – wasn't so dreadful and as I got to scribble loads of doodles I was happy. The structure of the course was to discuss the wider climate change picture and then we began to narrow it down to our own businesses to see if and how we could improve practices. I'm only half way through, a few more sessions at Eden and some site visits to other delegates businesses to compare and contrast but so far it's proving interesting. The start of the course was a bit shocking, all the facts and figures, the rise of costs, the change in climate, the damage to the environment all of these things were alarming but they're not new. We know that the world has been getting hotter, that worldwide there has been a greater frequency of extreme weather events, that there is more CO_2 in the atmosphere and that there is a finite supply of fuel. All this we know and yet it still seems to be a remote issue. Maybe because the problem is the next step; we don't scientifically, categorically know what is causing the problem or what is going to happen next and we don't know, therefore how to fix it.

The Green Foundation makes the point that even if we don't know what comes next we can make a pretty good guess that globally it's going to get hotter which isn't good news for billions of people. Even if things got no worse than today, Bangladesh would still suffer country wide flooding, Australia would still be on a permanent drought footing, America would be more prone to massive tornados to name just three very large countries. Maybe we will cool down again but the link between CO_2 emissions and global temperature rises is pretty clear for the last few years. So if we want to cool down we have to reduce CO2 emissions. Which are, amongst other things, fossil fuels. Hard to imagine a world without fossil fuels though but I think we are going to have to try.

Wave your flags but don't shove them in my face

There's been a lot of talk recently of flags and English colonial oppression and a lot of it has been very aggressive and unpleasant. I'm a bit alarmed by this, I don't remember oppressing or subjugating anyone recently, although my boys may have a different opinion on this. I felt sure that my days of looting and pillaging where behind me and I can't remember the last time I sacked a monastery or annexed a country but I am a working mum and have been known to forget things. Although surely I'd remember oppressing all my lovely neighbours?

The fact of the matter is that I just don't understand fanaticism; I don't hold it against anyone who is fanatical about anything, it's just that I'm not. If it's a black and white issue I'll find the grey, if it's a clear cut issue I'll be waving from the blunt edged fence. I know I'm quite extreme about seeing both sides of nearly everything, fanatical some might say, but the majority of us sit somewhere in the middle of most viewpoints.

I mean, I know we're all individuals, each of us unique and special, but we're also pretty much the same. We're all roughly between five and six foot we have two legs and two arms all coming off our body in the same place with a sort of round head at the top. And in the same way that our bodies are pretty similar so too are our personalities and beliefs. Saints and sinners stand out simply because they are so different to the norm. Imagine a society full of fanatics but fanatical about different things, imagine if those fanatics hold opposing opinions, well we don't have to imagine do we, we know how violent and bloody that looks. So it's just as well that the majority of us bob along in the middle of the river. We need the saints and the crusaders no matter how tiresome they may seem. Can you imagine what it must have been like kicking along with Mother Teresa of Calcutta? You're all for a hearty meal and an early night but she's going to work on until she collapses. Please! Talk about making you feel bad. So if we get the saints we get the sinners and if we get the crusaders we also get the fanatics.

When I write this column I tend to write it to myself and it doesn't occur to me that someone might read it but today a complete stranger came into the shop and said she enjoyed the column! I was thrilled, I was more chuffed than Ivor the Engine and it was wonderful. Now I'm wondering though if some irate reader is going to start shouting at me for not understanding the terrible burden that they have endured. If they do I shall be calm and as the Nun's used to say "Rise above it." Mind you, I'll also be tickled pink that they read it!

Discussing the marvels of hidden science

Do you remember the spoof Star Trek song where Scotty kept singing out "Ye canna change the laws of physics!!" Well I think there are a few laws of physics that haven't yet been discovered. The first such law would be the one that produces an invisibility particle. The level of invisibility is directly related to urgency or gender. For example, my sons and husband can go up and down the stairs all day long and yet fail every time to spot the bundles of stuff that need to go up; their books, their clothes, things for the bathroom and so on. The same invisibility cloak affects drawers; drawers in fridges are particularly problematic as my sons don't seem to be able to see them to open them. Equally their bedroom chest of drawers, the cutlery drawers, their desk drawers all seem to elude them. I on the other hand can always seem to see the keys on the kitchen table that everyone else is wildly running around looking for; it just stuns me that I'm the only one that can see them. I'm also the only one that can see puppy accidents and dead mice brought in by the cats. Imagine that.

Of course this isn't the only law of physics that Newton missed. There is the law of attraction between metal and thin air. What else explains why when I leave a safe distance between me and the car in front it is always filled by another car overtaking me? It's as though they are sucked helplessly into the void, like a dying planet hurtling towards a black hole. I find this phenomenon is dramatically increased by the appearance of water, be it heavy fog or rain; my braking gap is invariable host to a further two or three cars unable to resist the space. Of course I keep having to drop back in order to re-gain my space until it gets to the point where I am about to prove Einstein's theory of space, time and relativity and I find that I've dropped so far back that I am now before the point where I started, having travelled for longer than it takes to do twice the journey.

The same laws of attraction seem to work on the laundry bin. It appears that an empty bin creates a massive pull on the lid as it seems no one in my family is able to remove the lid and put their dirty clothes into it. Instead I walk in to find a huge gravity defying pile of muddy rugby kits perched above the lid stinking out the bathroom.

And it's not just physics that needs an overhaul; biologists have also missed a few tricks. Did you know that most foodstuffs and drinks are blue, or at least they

96

are after a few weeks of neglect? Some go blue, some are hairy and some are both. There are times when I go into the games room in search of missing crockery and I expect to see Mel Gibson charging towards me shouting "freedom!" Leaving hairy blue mould behind, did you know it can climb? A cup with only 1cm of coffee can expand to the top with its strange undulating fungus if left undisturbed for a few months. I'm not sure why NASA wastes so much money looking for life on Mars, they should have a look under my husband's pool table.

Oh well, I wonder if you've discovered any new laws of physics? We should write a book!

Digging up St Austell ...again

There's a road I use nearly every day and it generally seems that the rest of St Austell also uses it. It's Tregonissey Road and as it serves as one of the main roads into St Austell from the north, the College, Poltair School and Carclaze School it can be pretty gridlocked around 8.30 and 3.30. So I was a bit disheartened a few months ago to see the surface covered in white and yellow road markings, indicators of imminent roadworks. Still the summer holidays were approaching, of course, the obvious time to do the work. Now we're into the first week of August and nothing has happened yet, I hope by the time you read this the works are underway because it isn't a well-used tourist route so it won't cause undue traffic chaos but if they wait until September then what a mess that will be.

Of course it has always been a long standing complaint that highways and the utility companies seem incapable of sensible timing when it comes to digging up roads so I wouldn't be surprised if they do wait until September to start digging up the town's busiest school road just as the new term starts. It was clearly some sort of bonkers logic that decided that the best time to once again massacre St Austell high street was the summer holidays.

99

I couldn't believe it when I walked in the other day. Just how many times has the high street been dug up in the last ten years? It's truly ridiculous. Now it's been patched up with great big splotches of tarmac between the herringbone pavings. Presumably this means that at some point it is going to be dug up again or the whole road is once again going to be re-laid. Or maybe the council will run out of money and we'll be left with a patched up eyesore for another few years. It makes me really cross that no one seems to consider the impression that this gives to people visiting St Austell. Yes we have a nice new shopping area but there are no independents in there. The independents are what give a town its character. Holiday makers visiting Mevagissey are always commenting on how nice the local villages are but what a shame about St Austell. They all go to Truro instead. All those people visiting Eden and Heligan and yet year after year they pop into the shop and say "I see St. Austell is still a mess." I am beginning to hear compliments for the new development and that is encouraging but I care more about the independents and keeping profits local.

And of course it would be great for us locals to have a lovely, vibrant town centre but we can't ignore just how much money comes into the county during summer and how much St Austell misses out on.

Hey ho. I'm sure digging up the high street in the summer holidays makes sense to someone. Maybe some little A4 posters explaining the mess and outlining the benefits? Something in the newspapers? An explanation, an apology? A decent high street? Dream on kiddo and watch out for roadworks in September.

Things I've Learnt

I've been learning lots of things this week some you probably already know but I thought I'd pass them on anyway. The first follows on from my article last week about beach safety; I was sent a video clip this week showing what drowning actually looks like. I had always thought that I would be able to spot a drowning person; they would be floundering, calling for help, splashing about and generally drowning. The clip showed footage of a swimmer drowning, surrounded by other water users; this person was saved by the fact that life guards know what to look for. Someone who is drowning generally doesn't realise they are in trouble until it's too late for them to call for help. Their body becomes perpendicular, and their arm movements become small and shallow. They start to bob under the water and the body starts to close down the speech functions so that it can concentrate on getting air into the lungs. This usually only lasts about 90 seconds and then they simply slip under the water and drown. I was stunned when I watched the footage, the swimmer seemed fine, just a bit quiet and still. The best advice from lifeguards is if you see someone quiet in the sea in a vertical position to ask them if they are OK, if they don't reply, they're not. Get over to them, wave for help and tilt them onto their back. Once they can start to get air into their lungs again they quickly recover.

The next thing I learnt won't save any lives but it might save you some money and points on your licence. Friends had been out walking and when they got back to the car it was obvious the driver was pooped. Her friend offered to drive knowing that she had comprehensive insurance. Like me she thought she was also insured to drive any car. When she was pulled over by the police she discovered this wasn't the case. In the past we tended to get automatic cover for third party on other cars but gradually that element of our insurance has been withdrawn. If you think you are automatically covered to drive other cars third party you might just want to check. She got a fine and three points for driving without insurance.

The final thing I discovered was that English wine is now not just palatable but really rather tasty. No longer do you have to sip it in trepidation and then summon a winning smile and positive adjectives whilst wondering where you can spit it out. I visited the launch of a new winery and vineyard near Trethurgy – yes I know it sounds unlikely but they were seriously impressive. They have small vineyards dotted all around the area including a large one down on the Roseland. To date they have made two whites and a rose and all were very pleasant. In fact an open bottle was an empty bottle and if great wine wasn't enough they also cook up some pretty fine dining. The only dampener on the day was some chap who listened to the winemaker's talk and then said rather pompously to his own crowd, "the chap doesn't know what he's talking about." Obviously this was nonsense, as Knightor Vineyard are doing amazing things but I have learnt over the years that some people can only makes themselves look big if they are putting other people down. Still I guess that's not news to you either.

So that was my week and if the sun doesn't make an appearance soon next week's column is going to be all about the appalling state of my vegetable plot.

My lamentable vegetable patch

Whilst the country strives towards excellence and basks in the warm glow of a world's admiration of our fabulous Olympics and Para-Olympic games I feel the need to discuss something of greater importance. A matter of such significance that it has exercised my mind for the past four months and that Dear Reader, is my vegetable patch. It's hopeless. I mean really and truly awful. We had that fabulous, beguiling, deceiving weather in March and we rushed out to the garden and dug vegetable beds. In went the posts and paths, out came the weeds. Up went the poles for the peas and beans, in went the scarecrow. In the greenhouse we cleaned down the glass, we sowed our seeds, potted out the tomatoes and sat back in the glorious sunshine and reflected on what an incredible crop we would have this year.

Then came awful April, followed by miserable May, are you joking June, just about had enough of this July and here we are in August. My runner beans have stood still, my onions bolted, my potatoes got blight, the Quince dropped all its leaves, the courgettes shivered, the strawberries were small and white and my peas were pathetic. My grape vine has produced nothing. It's so disheartening; you expect some crops to fail but my sweet corn is only a foot high, my runner beans are not above my hips and have no flowers. Not that there are any insects around to pollinate them, all that ones that woke up early in March seem to have fallen by the wayside. My bumble bee nest has buzzed away, hopefully to a warmer spot and it's been months since I've seen a wasp or a butterfly. Winged critters are in short supply but rest assured the slugs are fine. In fact my one and only success so far has been my broad beans. They've been lovely and I'm eating them by the handful, my favourite way to have them is fried with butter, garlic, chorizo and scallops. Delicious!

But what can you do? I can't ask the heavens to stop raining. I can't ask the sun to shine and trigger my plants' photosynthesis, I'm tempted to take a hairdryer to my poor shivering strawbs as the soil is just too cold. I'm just glad that I didn't bother with many root crops this year, I don't think Unwins do a line in aquatic carrots or parsnips but if they did they'd make a mint. Maybe I should have tried water chestnuts and watercress?

So now we are in August and whilst not delivering great heat or high levels of sunshine it is a bit of an improvement on the last few months. I may get a few crops yet but I don't think I'm going to have a glut of anything. I hope that you've all had a greater share of success than us and if you do happen to have a glut of anything we will happily take it off your hands. Not green tomatoes though, I suspect I'm going to be fine there. Anyone got any good recipes for green tomato chutney?

Our beautiful, filthy seas.

What a week! My column on my rotten veg patch clearly hit the right note with you lot. Janet said that I made her feel better that she hadn't got around to doing her patch at all this season. Trevor pointed out that I shouldn't expect anything more as I lived in St Austell; everyone knows Meva has the better soil and Gemma's mother clearly took pity on me and dropped in a bunch of rather nice looking, and tasting, cucumbers! I often get feedback on my columns but a bag of veg is the best yet. Given my awful spelling I should be grateful that it wasn't a bag of rotten potatoes. I often get people telling me they read my column every week, they don't say they like it, just that they read it – I'm guessing that this lot enjoy the grammatical howlers and schoolgirl spelling errors. I hope I manage to disappoint this week!

Mevagissey played host this week to an Antarctic Island called Nowhereisland – it's floating around Britain as some sort of art installation. Quite frankly it floated in and floated off to Falmouth and I'm still not much the wiser about what the point of it was. Part of it seemed to be interested in the melting of ice caps, other parts were about becoming a citizen of a new nation and what that nation should stand for. Dave, in his rather down to earth way, said that we should focus on getting our own nation right before fixing imaginary ones.

The thing that has really caught my attention this week though was the stranding of the 50ft fin whale on Carlyon Beach. There was a lot of criticism on Facebook of people posting photos but I thought that was completely understandable. If I had been able I would have gone down to have a look because quite frankly I'm curious and I don't think there is anything wrong with curiosity. Where would mankind be without it? I should have loved to be able to see such an incredible animal up close. It was very sad that it died but it proved a salutary reminded of just what goes on in our seas out of sight and too often out of mind. Our seas are viewed as some sort of giant garbage dump but it is home to stunning leviathans, rare creatures, exotic, alien life forms even our weekly fish suppers.

So please don't dump your fishing tackle over the side for fish to drown in, keep your plastic lager ties in the bin as they get stuck on the noses of sharks and dolphins damaging their sensor systems. Don't get involved in balloon races as turtles can't tell the difference between jellyfish and plastic bags and balloons. They eat them and then die, autopsies showing stomachs full of plastic.

Get involved, join a beach clean, take up diving and visit the wonders of the deep for yourself or just simply aim to eat fish once a week and make it something other than cod; any fishmonger worth their salt will be able to give you some quick recipes. Our oceans are stunning and we are hugely lucky to live so close to the sea, we just need to pay it a bit more attention.

Foul, invidious league tables

Is there anything more insidious than a league table? The glory of being at the top, the shame of being at the bottom. Those at the top will happily declare it's a fair system and clear for all to see; those at the bottom will try to explain why their circumstances skew the figures. In the past, league tables never seemed to matter, unless of course you were of a sporting persuasion but over the last decade league tables have sprung up everywhere. Who has the best council, best hospital and best school? At least in a football match the league table made sense; score goals, go to the top, failed to stop goals, go to the bottom. But league tables for schools? How can you judge how one school is better than another?

At first it was simply done on who got the most children passing the most amount of exams. So stage one was already widely flawed and open to interpretation. Then they added a "Value Added" column this indicated how much   progress a child had made from their previous school. Unbelievably nebulous. Now they've decided that the initial measure of how many exams they were passing, failed to show the right sort of passes, so they've brought in something called the English Baccalaureate.

The EB is achieved if a pupil passes six subjects with an A* – C grade but these six subjects must be English, Maths, two sciences, a language and Geography or History. Previous exam grades had been five passes A*- C in Maths and English and any three others. These three others could include ICT, Child Care, Health and Social Care.

So what has been the effect of this new column? Well, it seems that schools that had a pass rate of 50% now have a pass rate of 18% suggesting that the majority of schools have pupils that are taking more of the modern subjects. Some critics are up in arms about this apparent slump in attainment, some seem to be suggesting rather quietly than these modern subjects are easier than the standard history or chemistry but I don't agree. All exams and syllabuses are set to the same standard, to suggest otherwise denigrates the efforts of pupils and teachers to get students to pass. Maybe more children take and pass child care rather than chemistry because it seems more relevant and easier to get a handle on? If I had been offered photography or physics at school it would have been no contest.

But what is the long term cost to our society? Shouldn't we be educating our future generations in as broad a spectrum as possible before they start to settle into their career subjects? A population that hasn't studied history is doomed to repeat past mistakes, knowledge of geography helps people to understand the world around them; the same is true of science, by knowing how things work helps people to look at issues and problems with greater clarity. A foreign language helps to broaden the horizon and consider other cultures as well as our own. I have no issue with the modern subjects but I believe the traditional ones give us a population that is more roundly educated about their heritage, the community they live in and the world around them. After 16 they can then continue down an academic path or a practical one but on either path they will be more roundly educated.

Doing battle with the green eyed monster

Doing battle with the green eyed monster at the moment. I think I'm winning but every now and then it grabs me by the ankles and trips me up. Whilst I'm lucky in so many ways and have so many things that half the world might be grateful for I can't help but look at those with more than me and think envious thoughts. Which is silly because I already have so much. But the start of the holiday season always seems to kick it off as I look at those lovely brand new cars towing jet skis and the like as they overtake me on the A30. Wandering around Truro in my walking boots and dog walking coat I look at families dressed to the absolute nines and think that it would be nice to dress my children in the latest styles (well it wouldn't because they'd either rip them, stain them or grow out of them before I could blink an eye) but it's nice to fantasize.

The problem with living in a tourist area is the sudden influx of people who view our home as a holiday resort, so of course they're dressed up to the nines, they have literally pushed the boat out and like all of us on holiday they spend money with ease. This doesn't mean they have lots of money on a day to day basis just that they have saved up and are now spending. They probably don't behave with such financial abandon at home but that's not the image I see. I just see the "what the hell, let's have another one..." and so I get a little green.

Of course the thing that makes me really green are the second homes. Now let me make things really clear, I have nothing against second homes in principle, good grief if I had the money I'd have a second home in a heartbeat. My second home would be on the Lizard, oh and one up on the north coast, and one on the Norfolk Boards and one near Cley. The point is, oh I forgot the one up in the Hebrides, and finally one on St. Martins; that's St. Martins on the Isles of Scilly not the one in the Caribbean. Oh what the hell, I'll have one there too. Whoops less of a second home more of a holiday portfolio. I guess my point is that those with second homes really do have more money than me and every so often I have little human moments and think "not fair." I think it in a very small voice but I still think it. It's then that I have to get a grip and remember what I say to the boys, we are happy and we are healthy, if we had to drop one of those to be wealthy which would it be? Of course my boys are smart and point out that you can be wealthy, happy and healthy, at which point we all sigh.

And as we sigh, we collect the boys from school and head to the beach to catch some waves and have barbeque tea. Or we scramble over the moors, not caring what we look like as we explore waterfalls and stone structures. Or we breathe deeply enjoying the sun above us or the wind in our face and the glorious surroundings that we live in every day and our sighs get a little less envious and a little more contented.

Of course if anyone out there reading this has a spare second home they no longer want, I'll happily take it off their hands.

Bring me sunshine, in your smile

When you're smiling, the whole world smiles with you. About a month ago a chap came into the shop sporting a very dour expression whilst wearing a t-shirt with the instruction "Smile" emblazoned upon it. I had to wonder if it was an aide memoir to himself or an instruction to others. Either way the contrast made me grin. A week or two later another chap came in smiling and telling me that it was his mission to make people laugh and proceeded to tell me a rather bad joke. It certainly made me smile. Then finally the other day at ASDA filling station a car pulled along side my pump and the chap jumped out and smiled at me, so I smiled back. Rather charmingly he said that mine was the nicest smile he received all day, so of course I grinned back even more. He laughed and said that he said that to everyone and he would also get back a full beam, belter of a smile rather than the original polite British smile. It was a fun exchange and not one that I was expecting whilst pouring loads of money into my heap of a car.

It was a strange month for smiling strangers, I don't normally get that many comments on my smile, possibly because a lot of the time I don't have my glasses on so I can't see anyone and if I'm thinking of something I have a rather vacant gormless expression or if it's a problem then I look akin to a bulldog chewing a wasp and is not very impressed with the situation. So when I do suddenly smile and my face emerges from idiot savant to grinning idiot maybe it's not surprising that it's commented on. Maybe I'm scaring people. Maybe they're just being nice to me whilst wondering how they can get away from the schizophrenic maniac.

However, it's nice to get a compliment no matter how startled it may be. Living in a house of boys these are few and far between. I tend to get comments like " but we love you?" as though to ask why should I need someone to comment on my new skirt. It's that whole gender divide thing with a gulf of misunderstanding in between. About a month ago I treated myself to some rather snazzy large green sunglasses – they're gorgeous. We were all off to the beach so I popped them on, full of self-pride. My husband took one look at them sniggered and said "Don't they make you look like Timmy Mallet!" Crushed, I slinked into the car where my boys also started laughing. Surely they had no idea who Timmy Mallet was? Indeed they didn't and they certainly didn't need to rely on their father's comments when they had their own opinions. "Hey Mum, you look like a frog!" We drove to the beach with three happy people and one rather fed up amphibian. My youngest boy must have noticed my dejection because as we got to the beach he sidled up to me, held my hand and whispered, "You don't look like a frog. Frogs are a different colour!" and suddenly I was smiling again, as compliments go it's a weird one but I'll take it!

So this week I'm going to smile at more people, I may scare some but I may also get some smiles back.

124

Why are holidays so stressful when you take the car?

Flick. And just like that the switch has been flicked and Cornwall has swelled to twice the size. You queue to get into Asda, you queue to get out again, you watch in bemusement as caravans get stuck. You notice that Tesco's has started to stock Pesto again and that your local newspaper has sold out before you get to it. Half term always seems to catch us on the back foot but like the migrating geese, instinct kicks in and we start to adapt. Back onto the back roads, up a bit earlier for the morning paper, going to Asda in the sunshine (everyone else is on the beach).

My bookshop is in Mevagissey, the lane outside my shop is cobbled and within 10 yards is the sea. In winter I listen to the gales, the rain, the seagulls, the peace and the quiet. In summer I listen to the laughter, the shouts, and of course the seagulls. I love this village and I love my life, I too, would come on holiday here but I can't help but feel sorry for those poor holiday makers who've spent four hours stuck on the M5 engines humming, fumes swirling, temperatures rising, spirits falling. Who would enjoy that? Eye spy becomes tedious after 30 minutes, even a teenager can't text for a whole four hours. Your eight year old boy who is a restless chap at the best of times has already attempted to chew his way out of the car after the third hour. Then having sat on the M5 in a heat wave you arrive in Cornwall five minutes after the heavens open for six days of non-stop rain. The sun comes out on the seventh day – just in time for the drive home.

I know some holiday makers are determined that every second counts and wake up and drag their fractious, fed up children back into the car in search of character building exercises. If children knew who Torquemada was they might think he was alive and well and building cars. But I think the ones that have got it right are the ones that just arrive and stop. They stay where they are and spend the first day resting; either kicking a football around the field, wandering down to the beach and jumping over the waves or just grabbing a book to read. There's so much to explore and do in Cornwall but one of the truly marvellous things about it is how very, very relaxed it can be. Just so long as I can get my paper, don't have to queue in ASDA and don't get stuck behind a caravan on the back road to Pentewan.

All this talk of holidays has made me want to start planning mine. I bet the boys would enjoy climbing Ben Nevis. It'll be good for them. Especially after a 10 hour car journey!

- This week I've been reading Of Mist and Bees, a bewitching fairy tale of family secrets, drinking Explorers Marlborough Sauvignon 2009 and listening to Story by Leddra Chapman. All excellent.

126

Well flaming June was well named wasn't it?

Flaming awful! Apparently it was the wettest June ever (well it certainly seemed it), the coldest June since 1991 and the dullest June since 1909, these figures are an average for the whole UK, how we fared in Cornwall hasn't been established yet but I can't remember a more hopeless month. So with that in mind I am packing to go on holiday, I'm taking my youngest son and we are heading off to sunnier climes. Well, we are heading off to the Peak District so maybe not, but we are going to travel with suitcases full of hope and optimism. We may return with suitcases full of mud and water but we're setting off in the right spirit. There is a saying that there is no such thing as bad weather just poor clothing and so out goes the bikini in goes the waterproof trousers. Away with the suntan lotion and in with the wellies. Sunglasses will be replaced with woolly hats and sleeveless blouses will be spurned for sensible raincoats and jumpers. I have checked the forecast and it's shocking so we are also packing playing cards, books, films and activity kits.

When we get a long run of difficult weather and although it seems unlikely right now, heat waves are also difficult weather, we tend to grumble at first, then get really fed up and then we seem to chin up and get on with it and I think the country is now entering a chin up phase. People had been putting things off but as the days have moved on but the weather hasn't, events have had to be cancelled or carried out regardless. I've been to too many events in the past month where people have enthusiastically commented on the fact that it's only a bit of drizzle, we seem to have given up on hoping for actual sunshine.

In fact it seems to be getting to a serious situation for those of us who benefit from the tourist trade and here in Cornwall I think that's the majority. I don't know the figures but it feels like there are fewer people in the county and if there are fewer people around then there is less money going into our economy. What I am hoping is that there are lots of people like me out there who just decide that they will make the best of it whatever.

I have a sneaky feeling that the Peak District will be wetter than Cornwall and if it chucks it down every day that will be a drag as we have loads of big peak walks and bike rides planned. Neither of us mind getting muddy in fact mud is something of a magnet but constant rain and zero visibility can dampen the most gun-ho of spirit. I had hoped to go pot holing but I suspect with this much rainfall it will be rightly considered too high a risk. There is Alton Towers but it's so damn expensive and throwing up in a roller coaster in the pouring rain having just spent £60 to get in holds little appeal, there is an outdoor swimming pool, which might have a novelty factor to it and will probably be empty and then there are the big stately homes that will be heaving with other damp, steaming families trying to entertain their disappointed and argumentative children; actually the more I type that sentence the more appealing throwing up at Alton Towers sounds.

Whatever happens I am going to love spending time with my son, exploring a new area of the country and hopefully not contracting pleurisy.

The Peak District or Cornwall?

It started badly. It started very badly indeed with me trying to lift two bikes, weighing 15 kilos each, above my head and then trying to fasten them to a bike rack. It was made worse by Steve trying to help. In a perfect world I would have happily stepped aside to allow the stronger person to do it but Finn and I were about to go to the Peak District on our own, and if I couldn't do the bikes on my own then Finn and I were doomed to spend a week just looking at two mountain bikes attached to the back of the car. Eventually with a scraped arm and covered in bike oil I managed it.

The next task was to drive the car loaded up, again it probably sounds daft to anyone that can pull a trailer, zip around the country with surfboards, roof boxes and bikes hanging of their car's extremities but I've never had so much as a comedy nose on my car. Off I set at three mph on a practice run certain that every speed bump was going to dislodge the bikes and leave them scattered across the roads ready to maim and kill everyone in my wake. Feeling vaguely confident that I wasn't about to create carnage I popped Finn in the car and we set off. For us things tend to be last minute, I don't mind this but it can throw up problems. Last year we travelled to Scotland in a car that we had only bought the day   before. This year we only managed to get the bike rack the day before, leaving us no time to test things out and fine tune them before the trip.

The journey north was wet and slow. It was slow because the rain wasn't helping and I was still terrified that the whole system was going to collapse all across the motorway. It took us eight hours to get there for what should apparently have been a six hour journey tops but to be honest once I entered the Peak District the roads become a challenge in themselves. Tiny lanes, sudden ravines, hairpin bends and lots of quaint villages oh and lots and lots of cyclists. Everywhere. Especially on every bend.

Something that the Peak District has introduced is a blanket speed limit of 50mph, no matter how wide and safe and rural the road, the top speed is 50mph. Given the types of roads and road users they have, this made a huge amount of sense to me and it got me thinking if Cornwall would also benefit from a similar restriction. Going to a tourist destination like the Peaks you can't help but draw other parallels with Cornwall. All in all they seem much more relaxed about their visitors, in Cornwall I sometimes think we are very up front and personal, sometimes too "in your face" if that makes sense. In the Peak District it was much more a "take it or leave it" attitude. There was no sense of bending over backwards or going the extra mile, sometimes it felt a bit brusque, other times it was nice and refreshing.

The thing that impressed both of us the most though was the area's attitude to bicyclists. There are trails everywhere to suit all abilities and all distances. There were extreme mountain bike routes and long distance routes over fifty miles, many of the roads had dedicated cycle lanes and all routes were well maintained and clearly laid out. Everyday Finn and I did about twenty miles almost exclusively car free. It would be nice to be able to do the same back home.

Philleigh Fair

Well I have just had a fabulous time with the family at the Philleigh Fair. It was full of simple pleasures and reminded me of how good things can be. I'm not a brown rice eating, macramé swimsuit type of gal but I do think that we are all fatter, lazier and greedier than we used to be. We want things and we want them now and we don't want to work hard for them – oh no – nor do we expect to pay much for them. And we're so impatient; if the phone isn't answered after five rings we're incensed, having to queue behind a whole three other people in the supermarket? Outrageous! Do you remember that lovely sketch in *To the Manor Born* when Audrey walks into her local village store that has now been turned into a supermarket. She proclaims loudly that if no one comes and serves her she will just have to help herself! So maybe we haven't changed all that much.

Funfairs just seem to be symptomatic of our modern greed and disillusionment, maybe the clue is in the word "fun" If a fair is proceeded by "fun" then you can guarantee it won't be. You will dish out £3 to sit on a ride which will literally reacquaint you with your breakfast two minutes later. A clever trick but not one I'm fond of and for what it's worth I find myself a little bit surprised that when I successfully throw a hoop, I don't win one of the big hanging dolphins that swing invitingly from the rafters but a scrawny looking toy whipped out from under the counter.

So I set off for Philleigh with a vague sense of unease but I should have noticed it was a fair not a funfair and it was brilliant. It takes place in one field, nothing is motorised, there is one steam engine playing tunes and that's it for mechanical moving parts. No candy floss, no scream if you want to go faster. Lots of screaming of laughter from the greasy pole though, cheers and clapping from the hay bale tossing, a coconut shy where the coconuts do fall off – but not when I was trying! And only 50p a go. The boys loved throwing tent pegs in a bucket – simple pleasures but it was harder than it looked, Steve liked the beer tent and Mum was taken with the sheep racing. Again I kept betting on the wrong sheep, clearly I am not a good studier of form.

My favourite event was the dog racing. The dogs chase a fox tail from one end of the track to the other, first past the post is the winner. Harry and I missed our race but we were told we could enter the next race. However, I was warned that whilst we were welcome to take part, the race was for long dogs. Ha! thought I, and yes, I did have an exclamation mark in my thoughts, if my Springer Spaniel couldn't beat a bunch of Daschunds then we were a poor show and no mistake. Oh the hubris as I walked onto the race course to find Harry and I surrounded by whippets, greyhounds and every other version of the Ferraris of the canine world. Ah, those sorts of long dogs. It would be fair to say that we didn't win, in fact Harry was so nonplussed by all the noise and excitement that when the off was given, Harry, for the first time, sat at my feet and looked up at

136

me with tongue lolling as if to say – "Yes? Now what" He didn't budge a muscle, he just sat there with a happy daft smile on his face and to be honest I probably looked the same. I'll have to wait another year for the next Philleigh fair but it's going to be great.

This week I am unashamedly re-reading and thoroughly enjoying Riders and Rivals by Jilly Cooper, please don't think less of me – they're great fun, proper rotten baddies, plucky heroines and totally undemanding, happy novels. What more do you want on your hols?

A Country Wedding

Last weekend we went up to Dorset for a family wedding, Steve's cousin was getting hitched and we were all invited. As the invitation was being arranged between two male cousins I didn't have a clue as to details. What kind of a wedding was it, church, civil? Should I wear a hat? Are you sure the children are invited? Are we going to the wedding, the reception or the whole shebang? Is there a whole shebang? Steve looked at me as we drove up the A30 and thought I was as nuts as all the poor holiday makers that decided to try to enter Cornwall on a Saturday at 10am. It was a wedding! Just turn up and go with the flow. Fair enough but there aren't many weddings that I have attended where "going with the flow" was the order of the day.

So we arrived at his mother's at almost the same time as Sarah, Stephen's sister, coming over from Essex and already there was a great sense of occasion. The cousins all fell on each other, whilst we all fought over the iron that quite frankly deserves pride of place in a museum. Suited and booted we convoyed off to the village, speculating on the bride; farmer's daughter apparently but beyond that no one had actually met her. However, she was   marrying Shaun so she clearly had a good sense of humour.

Arriving in the small Dorset village we discovered the most wondrous site, on the green in the middle of the prettiest little houses was a great marquee, all the villagers were milling about in the lanes and little signs pointed to the church. It seemed that half the village were attending and as the Vicar stood up to welcome us we understood the reception. Claire was the daughter of a local farmer who had farmed in the village since forever; the vicar lived next door to the family and had known them all since year dot. Everyone really did know everyone.

It was a wonderful do and I kept feeling like I was stuck in the Archers, everyone was in their best bib and tucker and Steve's uncle looked remarkably good if somewhat uncomfortable in full morning attire. We'd been laying bets as to whether he would even be wearing a tie! Because it was such a community wedding there were loads of children and the church was noisy with chattering children and neighbours catching up. The songs were sang with lust rather than accuracy and one child that had been bribed with sweets to keep quiet managed to time her sugar rush to the moment when poor Claire tried to say her vows. When the vicar asked the   congregation to support Shaun and Claire through their married life, the three of them had a quiet chat and agreed that our "We do" had been a bit quiet, so, once more with feeling please. We nearly took the roof off.

The reception in the marquee was generous, informal and tasty. Shaun and Claire arrived on a sofa, on a trailer on the back of a tractor and everyone cheered them in. The children had become a single pack and had taken to running in the dry river bed, feeding the sheep in the next field and climbing over the tractor, cravats were removed, belts loosened, high heels swapped for flip flops and everyone laughed their way towards the evening disco to which the entire village had been invited.

I think Shaun and Claire are going to have a wonderful married life if their "go with the flow" wonderful wedding is any sort of yardstick!

Rainclouds and supportive families

So, there I was out on an early morning stroll with Harry, there had been a terrific load of rain and wind the day before but the day had started bright, blue and warm and I just donned a t-shirt and leggings and headed off up to the Tor. It was a gorgeous start, I was stomping off looking at how lush all the vegetation looked and Harry was having a field day bouncing around after all the rabbits; he would no sooner run one down to ground in a bramble thicket than another would pop up behind him and leg it across the path. Instantly, the present quarry was forgotten and off he dashed in pursuit of more exciting prey. We were having a lovely time with Harry acting the loon, the rabbits clearly having got the better of him and playing tag with great dexterity when I noticed a change in the light. Suddenly everything was glowing, the green was shimmering the orange moss was electric, everything had a wonderful glow and I was kicking myself for not bringing my camera. My dismay about the camera only lasted about two seconds though because I know full well what causes that sort of beautiful light. The sun shining on dirty great big, rain sodden clouds. I'd been too busy looking at Harry and the rabbits to look up but sure enough, when I did there was the rain cloud. It wasn't just black; it had gone that very special shade of blue black that you get to see so rarely. What a treat.

Suddenly the beautiful light dropped as the sun was swallowed by clouds and a strong wind swept in to replace it. I picked up my tempo; I knew the car was a good 15 minutes away no matter how fast I walked, would I make it in time? I tried to convince myself that the "moist" air was no more than mist and I had bags of time when the heavens just opened. There is something glorious about being caught in a downpour, and if you can't run for cover the inevitability of accepting your fate can be quite liberating. I had these happy, hippy thoughts for about a minute and then I was just cold and wet.

Do you know the ditty that says "a stranger came up to me and said "Smile, things could be worse" so I smiled and lo! Things were worse"? Well I must admit that was where I was, standing on top of a Tor where the tallest thing after me was the low lying heather in the middle of a storm hoping and praying that despite the size of the clouds that it didn't turn into a thunderstorm. I was feeling pretty exposed and not just by my sodden top and leggings. For the last part of the walk Harry is always on the lead and we have to get back to the car along a path flanked by bracken, but under the weight of the rain and the strength of the wind many of the plants had keeled over onto the path, so now I had a very concerned spaniel who had transformed into some over exited Arab shying at every frond. He's a lovely dog but he can be a dopey wuss. I had to coax, cajole, push and pull him through every clump. My leggings, already wet, were now saturated, my skin was beginning to absorb water and what water it couldn't take on rolled down into my trainers.

Eventually a wet smelly dog and driver made it to the car to return home to find the street bone dry. As I walked in, the rest of the family, sitting eating breakfast, looked at me, paused and then all very gallantly roared with laughter. Roll on August.

Incidentally, The Passage by Justin Cronin started really well. Very reminiscent of Stephen King, imagine The Stand or Firestarter, the ending wasn't so strong and I have a sneaky feeling that with so many unanswered question it may be the start of a series but it was still a great read.

Prevarications

There are times when I feel very sorry for my editor. Usually it's because she has to try to sort out my novel use of punctuation or tackle my curious spelling alternatives but every once in a while I will get a phone call from her that's very friendly but also slightly strained asking where my article is? Today is one of those days. It's not so much Stop the Press or Hold the Front Page but it's quite close to Get a Bloody Move ON!

I'm afraid I have no excuse other than sheer indulgence. Towards the end of August I start to get so fed up with the crowds, the children and the business that I become as frazzled and bad tempered as an autumn wasp and last week I reached my snapping point. You are probably all aware of that moment where people who like you, start to talk to you in a careful manner and your partner tells you that you are unbearable. No? Oh, dear, just me then. Anyway it was time for me to take a chill pill. This advice was proffered by my youngest and rather than kill him I decided to do just that.

I've been out on two great dives out of Mevagissey. I love diving, it is so peaceful and so uncrowded, there is a whole new vista down there and you come become truly lost in your own contemplation of marine life. September is a lovely time to take up diving as the sea is warm and there is an abundance of plants and wildlife to look at. It's also nice to do an activity with a bunch of different people to the usual crowd; divers are always really friendly and because you are literally relying on your diving partner to save your life should anything go wrong you all get chatting pretty quickly.

As well as some great dives I decided to take Harry up to Minions and go for a really large, get lost type of walk. It was wonderful, I was out there for hours and saw hardly anyone, we discovered lots of new features that I had never seen before, ringed enclosures standing stone and so on, in fact Minions is rather littered with remains of archaeological significance, it almost seems as though it's hogging stuff, there is so much. Harry and I traipsed from tor to tor thoroughly enjoying paddling through streams and rolling in the heather, I did more of the paddling and Harry did more of the rolling. I even discovered a fabulous quarry, a place called Golddiggers near to the Cheese Ring itself. In fact it is so close that I was a bit embarrassed that I had never found it before. It's a wonderful location and as I sat beside it in the sunshine I watched a small shoal of fish also basking in the sunlight, with Harry popping in and out to refresh himself. It was very tempting to go for a swim but I didn't have a cossie and I didn't want to scare the group of teenagers that were also enjoying this little haven.

Finally, I spent yesterday on the beach with about eight other families; the children all grouped up and had a blast and all the mothers agreed that back to school couldn't come soon enough. So there we are, no excuses but I am now fully rested and will start next week's column tomorrow and save my poor editor any further grief.

Back in the grime

It's been a while since I was last in London but I got back up there the other day. It's a lovely feeling as you step off the train in Paddington and breathe in London and then your whole body starts to tingle and you realise that the tingle has less to do with excitement and more to do with oxygen deprivation. In the next moment that thick, stale air hits you and then you get shoved by a commuter who has better places to be. Oh London! The hot wind of the tube trains, the sheer misery of lost and late people, the unending sea of bodies all pressing and pushing through the stygian sub terrain.

I went from thrilled to be back in London to foul tempered in about two minutes. An hour later I had a splitting headache, presumably through lack of oxygen and I have to tell you that my smiling strategy wasn't going down too well. There was only one solution as there always is when I first get to London – Liberty's. It's fair to say that taking your husband to Liberty's is not a smart idea, unless the cries of "How much?!" neither irk nor irritate you. Having failed to convince him that £24.50 for High Tea for one was a reasonable price, and to be honest I was struggling myself, I bought some gorgeous Christmas tree decorations and then we escaped to Tate Britain. I went for Tate Britain rather than Tate Modern because there is only so much "Call that art!" that a girl can take.

As we arrived at the Tate it turned out that the road had been closed for Burberrys' show for London Fashion Week. I've never been near an event like this so we hung over the railings and gawped at loads of famous people that we didn't recognize and found the whole thing very funny. The photographer bay was heaving with flashing lights and people shouting at other people to "look to me! To me! Lovely!" All these glamorous people and we didn't have a clue. Steve was unfazed by his ignorance and was happy delighting in the sheer beauty of the girls and my word they were stunning. Finally we spotted Andy Murray and left happy that we could finally tell the children we saw their favourite tennis player.

The Tate itself was its usual oasis of calm and splendour. I love escaping into galleries in London, they're free and empty and full of wonders. There's a lovely grand picture of some well-to-do posing for his portrait with his gun and his day's spoils in hand. I rather like the Springer in the bottom corner eyeing up the dead rabbit. I wonder who that puts me in mind of?

We finally left to grab a bite to eat before watching Stephen Fry at the Royal Albert Hall, the purpose for our jolly. It was a good show and we had cracking seats but I'm afraid my mind kept wandering as I kept looking at all the books on the stage set behind him – some very nice bindings there.

Unsurprisingly, for someone as in love with the English language as Fry, he overran; he had no sooner walked off the stage than we were up and running for the night train. No doubt we missed an intimate *tete a tete* as he returned for an encore and invited those remaining to become his best friends forever and stay at his Italian estate but we had a prior date with BR that could not be avoided.

And then it was onto the sleeper train. What a revelation for £69! That covers the journey, a bed for the night and breakfast, I was really impressed. So London and back in under 24hrs with an evening show to boot. I do miss all that London has to offer but I don't miss the crowds and my lungs and wallet are both rather relieved to be back home, here in Cornwall, where the heart is.

Live in the now

Obviously with last week's article running a bit close to the bone, deadline wise, I determined to sit down straightaway and write the next week's copy. That didn't quite happen and whilst I'm happily on time this week I'm not as early as I had wanted to be. Of course I have a whole list of excuses as to why this didn't happen but the main problem is out and out prevarication. I absolutely believe in doing things the minute they need to be done, I just don't seem to be able to do it. This week has been a timely reminder to live in the "now". My youngest son has just gone up to senior school and it seems like a whole part of our lives have finished. I spent quite a while worrying if I could have spent more time with both of them when they were little, did I teach them the right things, did I pay enough attention to their concerns. Naturally I suspect I could have done more but I bet we all think like that and probably what we did was just fine.

The important part was making the most of the time, at the time. The company I dive with have just changed their business outlook to concentrate on commercial

155

ventures as that is where they want to focus but also so that they can see more of their young family. Whilst I shall miss diving with them it is so clearly the right decision. It always sounds like a cliché ridden card but "live for today" is just so correct. You don't know what is around the next corner, you can be sensible and plan properly so that you are prepared for a range of scenarios but you really shouldn't overthink it because you can't plan for everything.

So am I living in the now? Hardly; I'm spending all my time worrying about whether or not I let my children watch too much TV as toddlers, should I have talked to them more as babies and so on. Then when I'm not worrying about what can't be changed I'm paralysed by fear of what might come. What if they don't get on in school, what if they fail their exams, what if they don't get into University? It doesn't take much in my mind before they're on drugs and I'm visiting them in prison. Actually it's not that bad, my biggest worry is what if I don't like their girlfriends? What a mess! I'm spending all my time looking forward and backwards and completely forgetting today. I bet I'm not the only one but whilst "live in the now" is easy to say it's a lot harder to do and as I have already pointed out I'm really good at prevaricating.

However, it's a sunny day, my children went off to school with smiles on their faces, I have a big list of things to do which I am steadily working through and I am about to tackle three jobs that I have been putting off since forever. I'm cleaning the oven, I'm clearing the garage roof and I'm emptying all the rubbish from the passageway behind the house. Not exactly clean jobs but I'll feel great when they are done. I'll let you know which of them I actually did next week

Hallowe'en

Well it's time for things to go bump in the night again. I love this festival and we always made a big thing of it when we were little. Coming from a Catholic background we were far more in touch with the concept of Satan and all his minions coming out for the night until the midnight bell rang, summoning all the souls back below and coming from an Irish family, the witches and little folk were also running amok. When I was little Mum took us to see Disney's Fantasia and they played Night on a Bare Mountain. Wow – there was my Hallowe'en up on the silver screen exactly as I imagined it every year, it was thrilling and terrifying at the same time.

Beyond all the religious and historical significance which of course stretch back past Christianity to Samhain, there was also the fun side of things; nothing was so thrilling as walking down a long dark unlit tree-lined drive to knock on a stranger's door and call trick or treat. Then home to eat a plate of fried brains and human guts. Great fun! There are those who claim that trick or treat is a modern Americanism, not a bit of it. It's a very old European tradition way back into the 14th century and probably before. After all life was truly scary back then, so sometimes it was nice to make fun of it and of course we were all far more religious back then as well as being more in tune with the changing seasons.

It bothers me to see children and teens abusing it by being rude or intimidating but it bothers me just as much when adults are rude and aggressive to those who call at the door. It's an opportunity for communities and neighbours and different generations to all meet each other on a fun occasion. One of the mothers on my road goes and "prebooks" all her children's visits, she asks if the neighbours are happy to be called on and leaves treats for them to hand to her children when they knock on the door. How thoughtful is that?

And it doesn't have to be complicated or expensive. Last year our eldest son went off to an arranged party leaving a disgruntled little brother behind. So armed with only a torch the rest of us got into the car and drove to the Kings Wood. Thankfully it's a walk we do often so despite the dark we didn't get lost. It was really good fun, strange noises would rustle in the dark, odd animal cries called out through the dark, every so often Steve would disappear with a scream as something gruesome dragged him off the path and from time to time our torch would "fail" and we'd have to walk in bible black darkness. It was the perfect sort of terror, lots of giggles, some nervous, some screams and then hot chocolate and marshmallows when we got home. This year we're going to go to the scream and skate at Eden but I bet we manage to fit in another night time fright walk, well we have to, the eldest insists!

I'm currently reading Pillars of Earth by Ken Follett and it's marvellous and I've just discovered that Channel 4 are about to turn it into a series. Talk about coincidence, but I won't watch it, it will spoil the characters in my head. I've put a link to Night on Bare Mountain on the blog so you may be transported to a night of terror and demons.

Broken down car

There I was at the level crossing, gates downs, clay train nowhere in sight so I thought I'd switch the engine off and listen to the radio. Eventually the train arrived and passed, the gates were raised and my battery was dead. No phone, no wallet, loads of traffic that I'm now holding up instead of the train but thankfully there was a garage right on the other side of the crossing. In fact of all the places I could have broken down at least I was right near help. So I nipped over the line popped in and asked for help. I explained I couldn't pay straight away but would call later. Less than five minutes later engine running again following a great jump start. Excellent, or it was until I got home and found that that had cost me £58. Standard call out charge apparently.

Now I know I should have asked first, I know that they are trying to run a business, but nearly £60 for a drive of less than 100 yards and two minutes labour? I doubt that they made any easier money than me that day. So I'm fed up, I'll never use them again and if anyone asks me my opinion of local garages I'll not be adding them to my list of good guys.

Which makes me wonder about good customer service. Maybe I'm being unfair, after all they came out and fixed my car, but if they had told me in advance what the cost had been, I'd have declined, found a phone and called Steve out. In straightened times, a smile goes a long way and costs nothing. Keeping your customers in the loop, giving them options, even if it might mean you lose the sale, will mean you'll gain their gratitude. Hopefully, they'll come back to you for something else or maybe they'll just tell others how good you are.

It's funny isn't it? I can't tell you which garage it was because that wouldn't be "fair", I can tell you about good service but not tell you when I feel let down. It's all part of our sense of fair play. I made a mistake by not asking the price, they gave me a service so to complain would be churlish. And yet... Still I'm glad that it's this way. I'd rather we all praised people to the hilt and named them but kept quiet about those we were less impressed with. But there's lots of companies out there, that play exactly by the letter of the law, 90 day warranty means just that if your washing machine dies at 91 days then tough. Or that the excess charge was clearly laid out on page 14 of the small print. I'm sure we've all been caught out and left to feel stupid about it but it does rankle.

Good customer care

I was grumbling last week about poor customer service so I'd like to right the balance and talk about good customer service this week. It only seems fair and I'd like to start with the same company that caused me all the grief in the first place. I'm still not going to name them because I don't want to draw attention to the initial issue but they must have recognised themselves because on Saturday morning there was a knock on the door. I wasn't home, (will the rugby season ever end?) but Steve answered it, to the owner of the company. Not a man that either of us had spoken to when trying to sort out the bill. He had seen the article, realised we were talking about his company and was horrified at the charging policy. He came with an apology, a cheque and a lovely attitude. At no point did he ask for a retraction or for me to write something about the refund. The refund was not for the full amount but for the excess which seemed right and proper, I had no objection to paying something for the service and as he said, for such a small job so close to home you use your common-sense and charge accordingly.

When I got home Steve told me about what had happened and I was thrilled. Not about the money and not about the apology but about the fact that there's a really nice bloke out there that cares about his business and cares about his customers and that he's prepared to take responsibility for when things go wrong in his name. I didn't write the article to get my money back, that's not what I'm about and so I'm going to give the money to the RNLI, as I've mentioned in the past my sister is RNLI crew so it's close to home and of course me and my family seem to spend half our lives in the water so it makes sense.

Good customer service always hits the right spot. Sometimes it's about going the extra mile, popping in to a customer's house after work to drop off the umbrella they left behind. Sometimes it means taking a financial hit; it might not be your fault that Royal Mail lost your consignment but it's not your customer's either, so refund them straightaway and then undertake the claim on their behalf. Other times it's just thinking about what your customer might appreciate; providing wellies when they stay at your cottage or presenting them with a birthday cake at the end of their meal. Recently on Facebook, Finisterre, a local outdoor clothing company asked for dogs to join their "wolf pack" it was a silly thing but lots of us had fun posting up photos of our dogs. The next thing I knew they'd sent Harry a dog biscuit in the post. A small thing but what a clever thing to do. I was pleased at such a friendly gesture and they now have my mailing details and someone who is well disposed towards them.

164

Even when times are tough we take more than just the price into account when we shop. A smile costs nothing and can be the difference between a repeat sale and a lost customer. So now I'm going to have to practice what I preach and start getting my grins ready for the hundredth person who tells me someone needs to tarmac over the cobbles in Mevagissey.

The city of St. Austell

Welcome to the town of St Austell; so we didn't win the city bid and not only am I not surprised I'm also not sure if the prize was that big a deal anyway. I understand why St Ashap's went for it and why they got it, they do have a cathedral after all, they must be thrilled to be finally recognized after all these centuries, and Chelmsford and Perth, the other contenders are really quite large, so they made sense too.

What it has done though is make us relook at our town and consider it in a positive light. It's been so easy to denigrate the place over the last decade. The rot appears to have set in, according to local gossip, when the council said no to Marks and Spencer and they went to Truro instead. I wasn't around then but I know people who used to shop in St Austell who started to shop in Truro but let's be fair, Truro may have a smaller population than St Austell but it has a far larger commercial centre in which shops can flourish. It has more open areas within the shops to have markets and street fairs, it was the county seat and had other reasons for people to visit; the cathedral, the law court, county hall, the theatre and so on and all of these factors must also have had a factor on where shoppers chose to spend their money. As I said I wasn't here at the time and this is one of those topics where I run the risk of being shot down as an outsider that doesn't know what they are talking about. However, looking at it dispassionately, having M&S would have been great but the argument that other big businesses followed M&S into Cornwall and into Truro doesn't really wash, where would they have gone in St Austell? Even with a brand new shopping centre we still don't have anything large enough for a second department store.

Maybe losing M&S created a loss of confidence in the town amongst the people of St Austell; lord knows the amount of times I hear that that decision was the wrong one suggests that people were very bitter and resentful about it. And it is fair to say that St Austell has undergone something of a steady decline over the last few years but I can see a town getting back on its feet. I went to a recent Chamber of Commerce meeting and it was a pleasant eye opener. I'm not a member but they had an open meeting where all businesses could come along. The Chamber held their hands up and said that in the past they had had issues but they were making a new start, that included a greater level of inclusivity and a more open a receptive attitude towards new schemes and businesses. One great new event is going to be the first St Austell Spring Fayre on the 28th and 29th of April so come and join us and let's see if we can get things moving.

Water and children is a scary mix

There are days when I can't get a handle on this column at all. No matter what I want to say, I can't seem to make it come out right or make sense of it, this week's topic is one that has been sloshing around in my head for a few weeks now and I couldn't work out what the "angle" was but I think I've found it now.

Just the other day a group of six 12 year olds swam across the English Channel; they took turns swimming a mile at a time and made the crossing in 13.5 hours. The only reason I came across it was because someone retweeted it on Twitter. I was amazed not only by the feat but also by the lack of coverage. What a fabulous story this could have been. Such endurance and teamwork and for a section of the community that are often vilified as hoodie wearing hoodlums. I scoured the internet news sites looking for the story and only managed to find a short paragraph in the BBC Bristol pages where our aquatic athletes came from. However, whilst I was trying to find more news on this story I stumbled across a far sadder story. Another six children this time aged 13 to 18 drowned whilst playing around a river bank in Louisiana. One of the boys slipped in the deeper water and as he couldn't swim, started to panic. None of his friends could swim but they all tried to save him and died in their attempt. All six.

The contrast between the two stories was so stark and yet I couldn't find a way to shape it. The majority of the channel swimmers came from independent schools, was that the story? In the last Olympics 34% of our athletes came from independent schools yet only 7% of children go to independent schools. There's a whole column there but not one that seemed relevant to these two stories. Then there was the fact that the American teenagers were all black and the Bristol children were all white. If there was an angle there I'd be blowed if I could find it. Maybe it was the fact that we don't do enough in our media to praise the efforts of teenagers but would rather focus on negative stereotypes. I must admit this was where I was going until I opened the letters page in the Cornish guardian to discover that Polkyth are considering the removal of the springboard from the swimming pool.

Suddenly the angle was so obvious that I was amazed I hadn't noticed it before. Children need to know how to swim! They need to be confident in water. Tom Daly started his Olympian career from a 1m board, the fact that there isn't a high board in all of Cornwall is another matter and if St Austell does get rid of their board there won't be a 1m board in the whole of Cornwall either. The loss of a diving board is not the loss of a swimming pool but it is the loss of a skill; it requires confidence and technique to go head first off the end of a sprung board. Even if that doesn't appeal, who can forget the fun of running, bouncing and soaring off the end? All children are attracted to water and we need to make them safe. From confident swimmers we may get channel swimming, record breaking Olympians but more importantly, we will not have grieving communities, struggling to cope with the loss of their loved ones who died trying to save their friends.

The good old, bad old eighties

Is it just me or have we all gone back in time? OMD and the Pet Shop Boys are in the charts, Michael Jackson is heading to Number One; students are rioting, the country is struggling its way out of a recession and a royal wedding has just been announced! All of a sudden I'm back in the early eighties.

Now don't get me wrong, despite the recession, the strikes, the war and the riots I enjoyed the eighties. Put it down to the blissful ignorance of being a teenager but life certainly seemed easier. Well it was, I didn't have to work and I wasn't responsible for anything more complicated than getting my homework in on time, learning the lyrics to the new Eurythmics single and choosing what make up to wear.

Of course things were tough; girls had to choose between ra-ra skirts and pompom skirts and boys had to look at them without laughing. Mind you, the boys had their jumpers tucked into their trousers and wore jackets with rolled up sleeves. The Don Johnson look didn't even work for Don Johnson. For those of you unaware of these "to die for" fashion items, a ra-ra skirt stopped several inches above your knees and had about as many ruffles on it as a Spanish castanet player's sleeves. It was a rare girl that could avoid looking like someone's loo roll cosy; I was not that girl. Still I did manage to avoid the pompom skirt. If the model on Just 17 failed to look cool then I knew that it was going to be a non- starter for me.

Unfortunately I wasn't able to exercise the same level of judgement when it came to make-up. I seriously thought gold, blue and pink eye shadow worn together with electric blue mascara and black eyeliner was really trendy. Well it may have looked trendy but it didn't look good. I don't know if it's better or worse but I also had outfits to match the chromatic nightmare. A huge, fake, fur coat in electric blue, concealing a pencil skirt in fluorescent yellow cord and a satin effect blouse in shocking pink. Nicely finished off in patent black high heels. It's almost impossible for me to imagine how bad I looked, were it not for the fact that my parents took photos. There we all are, beaming out at the camera, eyes and teeth as bright as our outfits, full of life and ready to take on the world. The fact that we looked awful and our parents must have been crying with laughter to themselves didn't matter a jot. We thought we looked great and we were having fun.

So when my son tries to wander out of the house with his trousers slung so low it's damn near indecent I can only be thankful that he doesn't have any electric blue pants!

Oh the joys of a long road trip with children

Me and the family have just returned from Wales, Pembrokeshire to be exact. A wonderful time was had by all but, don't fret, I'll spare you the details. I always remember my parents putting on a slide show, every year, of their holiday snaps. The neighbours would be invited around, teas and coffees dispensed and the lights dimmed. The clack of Dad's slide projector would be like nails in a collective coffin. Rictus grins would be fixed to bored faces and my father would keep up an interminable commentary.

Finally all and sundry would shuffle home, muttering that they'd missed the start of the generation game, dad would put the slides back into the box (after carefully labelling and numbering each one) and the rest of the family would breathe a sigh of relief, safe in the knowledge that we had another 51 weeks to go until the next time. Holiday snaps are only interesting to the people who were there; even I could see that from an early age.

Holidays rarely go smoothly I find. There is usually some fly in the ointment somewhere along the line. Packing is usually the first hurdle for us. This year I sent my children upstairs to pack their own bags. Big mistake. The youngest came down with a bag full of electronic gadgetry and games, a stack of beano's and a pair of pants. On closer inspection the pants weren't clean. I ended up doing the packing. Again.

I figured that with two young children on a five hour drive I would be sensible to provide some electronic entertainment for the journey. A five hour stint of I-spy is not my idea of fun. So I downloaded some films and audio stories to PSP's and Ipods. An emergency ration of sweets and comics was stowed aboard and, after loading the bags, an exercise akin to the krypton factor, we set off. Hurrah!

It was at Bugle that Steve realised that he'd left the mobile at home. We returned and off we set again. At the end of the road Steve again mutters those dreaded words "Oh hang on…" And so the cycle repeats and tempers are strained even before we have left St Austell.

Tempers are even more strained when we hit the first traffic jam on the A30. Never ever travel out of Cornwall in August on a Saturday. And always, always listen to the neighbour who dispenses this advice. What were we thinking? Films have been watched, comics read and emergency sweets eaten and we hadn't even got to Oakhampton. And then, from the back, bored children start squabbling. Boundaries are crossed with fingers or feet followed by cries of "get off my side". And then the question that all parents dread on long journeys, usually asked every five mins and beginning "are we nearly…" I can't bring myself to finish it.

But we finally made it. Our five hour journey turned out to be seven. And when we got to our destination, stretched aching limbs, yawned and unpacked we headed down to the beach for an evening dip. And was it all worth it? Absolutely! Would we do it again? Definitely – we still had to get home.

Now I didn't get a whole lot of reading done because I forgot to pick up my "to be read" stack but I did finish The Knife of Never Letting Go by Patrick Ness. Sort of fantasy but not really important to the main theme of the story which is about loneliness, bravery and what it means to go from boy to man. Unfortunately it was the first book in a trilogy – oh how that annoys me – so I'm now reading the next book to see how the story unfolds.

My depths of my stupidity knows no bounds

For the first time this year I have a friend coming no stay. No visitors before September is a thing unheard of so I'm really looking forward to seeing her. The thing is I've woken up with the plague, added to which it's the first week back at school and the house is a tip. Now I know that she's an old friend and has seen far worse and quite frankly wouldn't care if the place was on fire but I care. So I am trying to run around like a loon trying to make the place resemble a home you would like to stay in rather than a hostel you can't wait to check out of. Before any house proud zealot pipes up and asks why the house isn't always spik and span, the answer would include the words dogs, boys, back to school, business to run and go away. The problem with today's blitz is that Thomas hasn't gone back to school yet so is in the way trying to help and getting shouted at because as I mentioned before I have the plague. The plague struck

179

in the night, I kept waking up feeling a bit woozy and sniffy and just couldn't get back to sleep properly. When I at last got up I was sniffing and feeling a little pathetic and then looked in the bathroom mirror. Overnight my chin seemed to have developed some sort of festering sore that would have graced any mediaeval peasant's face. Well vanity, thy name is woman but I had too much to do, so off on the school run and the dog walk whilst trying to hide my face from anyone I might know, and anyone I might not, and small children, and animals of a nervous disposition.

The walk along the cliffs from Par to Polkerris was doing me the world of good but on my return I noticed that the air was full of buzzy things. Probably due to the plague, my imagination was beginning to get very vivid and with thoughts of recent wasp attacks I proceeded with caution getting twitchier and twitchier. Finally the path narrowed and the air thickened with all manner of flying insects and something buzzed right by my ear. Instinctively I went to swot it but forgot the dog lead in my hand. With immerse force I swatted the insect and smashed the metal ring of Harry's lead into my forehead. There was a moment of stunned silence and then quite a lot of colourful language and checking for blood. The last time I had been hurt this much was when I swung a windsurf pole into my head. If I have more brain cells I might stop to wonder why I keep banging myself on the head? However, as my brain cells are diminishing with each attack I fear I shall never know.

So here I sit, trying to get my column in on time, the house clean, surrounded by tissues, my head thumping and bruised and my face covered in sores. Reader, I look a mess! Hope you are all feeling better and I'll chat again next week.

Devon or Cornwall

We were in the audience at Plymouth Pavillions last night, laughing with Billy Connolly, when he started singing a song about the flowers of Devon. Devon! Why on earth was he going on about Devon and then the penny had dropped, we had left God's own country and crossed the border. I know that Plymouth has special dispensation for all those unfortunate Cornish children that had to go there to be born but in all honesty it isn't Cornwall.

Isn't it funny how each county gets proprietorial? Some counties seem rather relaxed about their identity but we know that's not the case here. It's not just those living in Cornwall that seem rightly fascinated with the county or country depending on your leaning but so does the rest of England. The media is full of Cornwall, every five seconds there seems to be another show based in Cornwall, recently we had Caroline Quentin frolicking around in holiday homes and the River Cottage boys foraging along the highways and byways. Next week Monty Hall is down at Penzance, Claire Balding is Rambling in Looe on Radio 4 and so it goes on. I can't think of another county that receives such constant attention. It's not just TV and radio though, every time I pick up a magazine you might be forgiven for thinking that the only stretch of coastline in the UK is down here. I've moved around a lot and whilst Cornwall does have jaw droppingly beautiful beaches we're not the only ones.

I'm not complaining and all the free publicity is great but the upshot is that everyone heads for Cornwall. Like I said, not complaining and I love the variety of people it brings into the county – you have to admit we're not the most diverse bunch of people but I just wish that it didn't cause so many issues. I was driving into Newquay last week and someone has posted a sign on one of the main welcome boards that reads "Be nice or go home." Now, I know that doesn't seem hugely friendly on first glance but is it that different to "Please drive carefully through our village"? It's just some local asking for their home to be treated with respect and courtesy – god knows Newquay is suffering at the moment. Long term residents must wonder at the planning decisions that have turned their town into a loud and filthy playground. So yes, please come and share in the beauty of Cornwall but please also, keep it beautiful.

At the auctions

If you ever go to the auctions and see a gentleman and lady silently bickering and giggling their way through the event, chances are you'll be looking at two of Hurley Books' finest. Steve and I both love going to the auctions but it would probably be better if we didn't go together. Last week I was after a lot of bird books, there were some really nice Cornish ones with line drawings that I particularly wanted but Steve couldn't see the attraction. Bidding had got to £30 and Steve said enough, I of course was happy to go on but the auctioneer had seen his emphatic shake, moved past us and finished the bid with someone else at £32. Steve then had to endure a silently fuming harridan stood next to him for the next few lots.

That's the joy and the problem of an auction. I was convinced that I could have had that lot for £32 but of course if I had continued to bid against the other person we may have gone way past £50, you just don't know how much the other person wants what you want.

We started to whisper again as we secured a few lots and the ones that Steve was keen on began to hove into view. We should have paid more attention because as the auctioneer called out lot 125, Steve groaned realising he had just lost his place and lot 124 had sailed past. Surely the hammer didn't fall on such a ridiculously low figure of £15? Please let it have been £150. Please let me not have missed the bargain of the century?

Then a collection of children's books was ready. Now this was a beautiful lot of Edwardian picture books including a Rackham. Guide price £80 -£120, well that was reasonable but I was prepared to go to £200 because there were some really nice titles and one or two I had never even seen before. So as the lot approached I braced myself ready for action; the auctioneer had some bids on the book and opened at £250. Talk about having the wind knocked out of your sails, it would seem that someone else also rather liked the look of those books.

The day wore on and we got most of what we had come for as well as a few speculative lots. These will be ones that we hadn't looked at but were going for such a low price it would be rude not to buy them. Collection at the end was funny, there were a few pleasant surprises and one or two groans but by and large a success.

Steve went to the next auction on his own and I nearly fainted when he came home and told me what he'd spent. Granted, he got some really fascinating things but oh mercy, our poor bank balance. So now it's noses to the grindstone, get the books listed and up onto the internet and into our shops, otherwise Christmas is going to consist of a lump of coal and half a carrot.

Farewell to the News of the World

Well, the News of the World is no more. I can't say that I will mourn it's passing other than the fact that it has been in print since 1843 and it always makes me pause to witness the end of an era. I find it interesting that what caused the paper to stumble was not the voyeuristic and illegal ends it went to, in order to titillate its readers but that it stepped over a moral boundary. I had begun to think that this country had no moral boundaries left. It wasn't the taping of phone calls that we objected to, it wasn't the invasion of privacy of some celebrity, it was the deletion of messages on a missing school girl's phone and the fact that this activity gave her parents and police hope that she may still have been alive. It was this act that sickened the nation because we all understand the fear and horror of losing a child and we all understand how desperately we would cling onto any tiny hope.

Do I think that News International have done the right thing in shutting down the News of the World. Actually, I don't. I think this was the most cynical act of "mea culpa", a dramatic whitewash. Who benefits by the closure of the paper? Certainly not the staff. Does the public? Well I don't think they care one way or the other. Do Milly Dowler's parents care and all the other people spied on? No, I imagine they would be more satisfied with legal prosecutions. So who does benefit? Well I think News International benefits from the closure. In the past six months alone the News of the Worlds sales figures have been about 7% down on the previous year, month on month. They haven't been alone in this; the circulation figures for all newspapers are in decline and it's no real wonder. As we become more online as a nation and satellite television brings us constant, up to date news channels, something has to give. Print media is just part of a long line of changes, record shops, DVD hire shops, book shops, libraries; they are all gradually being challenged, threatened and re-moulded.

The Murdochs must have looked at this awful fiasco and realised that there was a way that they might be able to regain some public sympathy and shore up their finances at the same time. They "nobly" threw themselves on their sword, whilst stabbing their employees in the back with the same sword and then cut away a loss making enterprise with a swift clinical detachment. Cynical? You betcha! I am glad to see that their bid to get the rest of the satellite market has been knocked back though. Looks like they haven't managed to glide through this untouched.

However, I'm not particularly impressed with the police in the handling of this matter either. To listen to senior officers in the Metropolitan Police Force say we couldn't pursue these claims because NoTW wouldn't cooperate are incredible. If I commit an illegal act and am accused of that act, then I'm thrilled to discover that if I fail to cooperate with a police investigation that the matter will be dropped. Maybe if I had close working links with the media and the politicians I would stand a better chance of getting away with stuff. It's not a nice thought but it certainly seems to be the case.

Hogwash to the lot of them!

Failing exams doesn't make you a failure

Putting dogs on the curriculum caught my eye in the paper last week as a rather odd sort of feature. It turns out that a local charity would like greater awareness of dogs, taught in classes. I don't know how they plan on running it, maybe a short course like the cycling proficiency test, not sure if they even do that anymore. My children never did one. Anyway, I digress. I like the idea of dogs in schools. Without a dog at home children may lack the opportunity of knowing how to approach a dog – or not! It would also be a safe environment for a child where they may have picked up fears from a parent and can approach the dog without pressure from a parent. Too often I see families on walks where the parent grabs a child and pulls them towards them or hides the child behind their legs. I know Harry can be a muddy brute but that's all he is. Those children are being taught that dogs are things to hide, or even worse, run from.

Close up lessons with dogs could also remove some of the shine from them. Picking up poo will harden all but the most enthusiastic dog lover and may spare parents the inevitable pleas at Christmas. Lessons aimed at teenagers may help to show how expensive and time consuming a dog is and how quickly they lose their cute puppy appeal.

All in all I think it is a good idea but to be honest our curriculum is already so crowded with other things and constant tests, that I don't see where it will fit in. If I had my way with the curriculum I would bring back all sorts of things like cooking and sport. Not food technology and sport science but actually putting stuff in an oven and running down a field. I'd have more outward bound type lessons and more making and doing stuff sort of lessons. I'd also have lessons on how to understand a bank balance and how interest works on a credit card. Instead of being taught how to use PowerPoint I'd want them taught how to write programmes. To be makers rather than consumers. Of course for the academics, our curriculum is fine, not brilliant because we don't push our smartest kids hard enough, but for our non-academics it's hopeless. Everyone is now expected to get a gazillion brilliant GCSEs and then race on to get even more wonderful A levels and then dash off to university and a whole pile of debt. But what about the excellent children who just can't do exams, don't like academia and just want to make and do. Where are our academies for inventors and engineers, our athletes and explorers? Right now they are probably at home feeling useless because they didn't get the GCSEs that society seems to keep saying is needed. Some of them will make it, those Richard Bransons out there will pick themselves up with no help from the current system and forge their own careers, but many more will feel worthless, maybe dreaming of easy fame but looking around them and realising that they can't do what society expects of them.

So yes, let's have dogs in the classroom and with their wagging tails let's have some more fun, and lessons where different types of kids get to shine and wag their tails as well.

196

Online versus high street

I'm part of an online community of booksellers and we regularly chew the fat and try to put the world to rights. One of our recent discussions was about someone's local bookshop that had just closed down. They sold new books, were in a prosperous town in a good location but had gone into liquidation. Similar tales were soon pouring in from all over the country.

Many things were to "blame," high rates, Kindles (electronic books) and of course Amazon and in truth all of these things are a genuine threat. I wouldn't run an all new bookshop if you paid me. How on earth do you compete with a business that can provide an almost limitless range, next day delivery and the cheapest copy? I know Mary Portas, (Queen of Shops) recommends reconnecting with the community, making your product and shopping experience unique and offering excellent customer service and of course that's excellent advice but the best bookshops have author events, affiliated reading groups, story times, coffee shops and so on but that still isn't enough. I don't blame Amazon, it's just a new development, of course not everyone buys online but that's the way the trend is growing and now you can download a book direct to a portable electronic reader. Personally I don't like the idea but boy are they popular!

We amble along selling a few new titles, local interest for example but mainly excellent condition second-hand books. We order books for customers new or out of print and we even do home deliveries, we have a regular changing stock and a friendly place to come into and of course we are situated in a very busy tourist centre, which probably helps more than anything else. We think we get it right most of the time but it's more often luck than hard work. Like most of the tourist villages in Cornwall, Mevagissey has loads of independents and it's fabulous. The staff are more often than not the owners and they know their products inside out. They care about what they sell and they want the customers to come back time and time again. And they do.

Look at St Austell town centre, how many independents are there? The town is finally growing again but none of the growth comes from local independent owners, over the last three years I've seen loads of small businesses open and close again which is heartbreaking when you think of all the effort those people have put into starting up their business. And I can't blame the customers, if the shop is offering the wrong product or too high a price who can blame them for choosing to shop elsewhere? But why can independents survive in Meva but fail five miles away in St Austell?

So let's have lower rents and rates in St Austell, in fact why not waive rates for the first year and let the business get established? A more diverse range of shops and attractions will bring in more shoppers and away we go.

Now talking of independents I had a nice glass of port the other day from Del Monicos called Double Diamond of all things. Much loved by alcoholics and underage drinkers alike, that double diamond was a fairly foul beer, this Double Diamond however, is a very quaffable port.

I'm also about to finish One Day by David Nicholls; it's an enjoyable read following two friends as they leave Uni. in 1988 and how their lives twist and turn. It's funny in parts and often I catch myself thinking "Oh god, I remember doing that!" I have a horrible feeling that it's about to end badly because everyone I've mentioned it to has gone "I loved that book but boy did I cry." I wouldn't have picked it up if I thought it was a weepy, I tend to avoid them. So I'm glad I didn't know it about this because I'm really enjoying it. Maybe we've already had the weepy part and I didn't notice? I'll let you know next week.

Mellow fruitfulness

Well autumn really came up on us quickly this year; the early hot spring meant that the harvest was also early. September seems to have consisted of nothing but wind and rain making the dark nights seem even earlier and the holiday makers have stayed cuddled up on comfy sofas leaving the streets and sights quieter than normal. All this early hibernation inevitably makes me think of winter and like so many of us I want to get the house looking nice for Christmas. Why Christmas when so many no longer celebrate it as a religious festival? It is because it is still a festival and has been for centuries before Christianity. It's around the shortest days of the year and it's the start of a new year. We get to pause, swop gifts, get together, eat well and so the dormice amongst us want to make sure that our little bolt holes are warm and snug for the celebrations.

It must be a maddening time of year for the trades and furniture suppliers with a sudden avalanche of orders all to be delivered, fitted and installed by Christmas. Part of the urgency is of course down to the fact that we know if it isn't in by Christmas we won't see hind nor hare of a fitter or delivery van until well into the second week of January. I imagine that I'm in a similar position to lots of folk in Cornwall, I make my money in Summer and I only have the time to spend it in autumn and of course if I'm buying a new sofa then I want it by Christmas so that I can loaf in front of my fire watching rubbish on TV, drinking something excellent and generally indulging myself. I don't want to be sat on my sofa that has given gallant service over the past 13 years but is now beyond repair.

The problem is finding a sofa that beats or matches the old one, and one that we can all agree on. The last sofa we bought was a stunner, we spent a lot of money on it and it was worth every penny. This, of course, was before the children had arrived and we had money. Over the decades it has been a bed, a castle, a trampoline, a submarine and the most comfortable sofa ever, very deep with huge thick feather cushions. Replacing it has proved hopeless, in the first place it's not something you can buy on the internet, you have to try it out and you have to try it out together. What I think is comfy, Steve thinks is ugly, what Steve thinks is perfect, I know won't fit. We wander around furniture showrooms with their gorgeous lounging sofas that would look great in a warehouse apartment but honestly how many of those are there around here. It's ridiculous, we have a nice large front room but I think a sofa longer than two meters will dwarf it. I wonder how many people get their sofas home only to realise that they can no longer close the door? So far the only ones we can agree on are the ones that we can also agree cost too much. Well the cost is relative isn't it? It's worth the money but we don't want to spend the money, so there we are. Maybe when the children have left home and we know it will no longer be used as a rugby touch down, a diving platform or a balance beam then we will indulge. For now though I think it's going to have to be something that will do and be in by Christmas. Maybe I'll buy a nice rug to throw over the fake leatherette and cuddle down into that instead. Or maybe the sun will come out again and I'll forget all about winter and leave it until the last minute.

A busy week

And then there are weeks when I've done so much I don't know where to start. Saturday was particularly crowded, the day started with my youngest son taking part in the St Austell Music and Speech festival, he was competing in the Grades One & Two piano section and once again overcame his nerves to do us proud. This annual event always seems to have low attendance figures and yet the standard of performances throughout the week is always excellent. It's a great opportunity to hear stunning music at close quarters for a £1 entry fee. So my thanks as ever go to the organisers of this event and to his piano teacher Rachael Mitchell.

Having dashed out we then sprinted over to rugby practice at Lankelly Fowey, again another bunch of incredible volunteers who run the most friendly, welcoming supportive club around. Unfortunately, due to bad weather the following day's match against St Austell had to be called off, funny matches are often cancelled but never training! As soon as that was finished my youngest son was whisked away to a birthday party at Retallack Lodges to go on the Flow rider. It's hard to explain the flow rider unless you see it but try to imagine an upside down wave on a trampoline. So whilst he went off to defy the laws of physics, Steve and I scooped up our disgruntled eldest son and dashed over to Meva to set things up for EV Thompson who was coming to the shop to sign copies of his latest book "Beyond the Storm." As usual, he arrived on time and was promptly inundated by friendly fans and we had a great afternoon. He's a lovely man and I enjoy meeting him every time. I'd also like to say thank you to all the people that chose to buy his book from us, we appreciate the support that you give us and it's always nice to meet new customers.

Of course that wasn't the end of the day as Mevagissey switched on their Christmas lights and it was a wonderful event with a lantern parade and stunning light puppets all marching to the beat of a Celtic samba band. So yet more thanks to the committee who despite really challenging conditions this year put on a memorable event. And whilst we're thanking people, thank you for everyone who is still shopping in Mevagissey, almost all of us are open for business and it can be lonely if people think the village is still closed.

Sunday was a true day of rest. Tuesday however saw us carefully bombing up to Bristol to wave goodbye to my sister as she prepared to sail across the Atlantic. Thank you to both of the boys' schools for knowing that there are more important things in life than attendance figures and thank you to the meteorological gods for giving us such an amazing display of hoar frost as we travelled up country. The highlight must have been hitting -10 at Okehampton.

Wednesday found us jumping up and down to three rappers at Plymouth Pavilions who were warming the crowd up for Diversity, the dance act that won Britain's Got Talent last year. It was amazing, I went with friends and seven boys ranging from eight to eleven who loved it even more than we did.

By Thursday we were all a bit tired and blurred around the edges but carrying on, and now today we will end the week with the school's carol concert. In amongst all this we have been preparing to launch our new website which I'll tell you all about next week. So there we are, a properly busy week and thanks to everyone who made it a great one.

A thousand and one frustrations

Well it's been a week of little frustrations. I ordered some books for a birthday present for one of my son's friends. I ordered a special next day delivery so that they would arrive in time. Ordering books is something that I'm pretty good at. I'm used to it. What I'm not used to is delivery companies failing to deliver. I would say that 99% of my deliveries arrive without fuss or fanfare but the 1% that don't turn up when you want to? Well, you can guarantee that they are the ones that are time sensitive. So of course these books failed to turn up on day one, day two or day three, the party came and went and there's me, a bookseller, unable to provide books for a birthday present. Only mildly annoying then.

Talking about the shop, our scaffolding is still up, not the end of the world and it does mean that the work is getting done. Well our work is all done but our neighbour has bigger problems so we just have to wait. Hardly his fault and it needs to be done properly but you know how it is. It still irks. I want to show off my newly painted shop to everyone. Which leads me to my next frustration, my scaffolding is up but my Christmas decorations at home still aren't. A leak in the house has meant that our sitting room ceiling is sagging. We got a plasterer in to have a quick look, he took a quick look and then he left telling us that what I thought was a quick dot and dab job, was actually going to involve taking down the coving as well as a good portion of the ceiling and to call our insurers.

So now I am waiting for the loss adjuster, talk about spirally out of control. And whilst I wait we can't put up the decorations, well what's the point if we have to take it all down again. We can't dress the tree or deck the hall and our fa la la la la is definitely out of tune. Little things really can grind you down and then in amongst all the stupid minor inconveniences comes an act of an utter pettiness and you wonder why they bothered.

My mother went to catch the bus into town the day after her birthday. Now it may shock you to discover my mother has a bus pass, well it does me, it means I'm not 18 anymore but that's one of my other minor frustrations. Anyway, she got on the bus, handed over her bus pass and was told it had expired yesterday and had to be withheld. Furthermore if she wished to travel into town she had to pay. As she didn't have her purse on her she had to step off. Now I ask you? What was the point in that? It's not as if her birthday made her a year younger and no longer eligible for a bus pass. Why couldn't the driver simply have told her that it had expired and that she needed to refresh it? Why treat her like some sort of fare dodger? My mother wasn't bothered, she just brushed him off as a jumped up jobsworth but I got annoyed on her behalf.

So there we go a week of niggles and frustrations. Next week will be a doddle. Ho ho ho!

Cooking the Christmas Cake

Once again cooking the Christmas cake led to family rows and it was all my fault. For some reason I expect my family to all gather round as we chop the peel and tell jokes, Bing Crosby hands out the sherry and King's College, Cambridge join in on the songs. Snow gently falls against the window panes and we warm our hands by the fire. I know I'm raising my expectations too high and I have no issue with high standards, it's just that when they unsurprisingly fail to deliver I'm disappointed. I may be able, somehow, to get one of the most beautiful choirs in Britain to squeeze into my kitchen, I may even be able to raise crooners from the grave but snow? In November? In Cornwall? Some miracles even I can't perform. The other miracle I can't perform is to get my boys to stay in the same room for longer than 30 minutes without fighting, so then I get crabby and then they get crabbier and Bing Crosby is grabbing his coat and high tailing it out into the rain.

Anyway, by the time the cake was ready to bake I had left it too late, of course that didn't stop me and in the oven it went. A potentially huge mistake as two hours later I really needed to go to sleep and the cake still had a good hour to go. In desperation, I turned the oven down to .5 and went to sleep wondering what I would come down to in the morning. Sometimes though life is on your side, we all woke up to a house smelling of brandy and cloves, fruits and nuts and just the very essence of Christmas.

The reason I'm waffling on about the cake is how important cooking is in a family. My youngest son's school had a baking day last week. Virtually the whole day was set aside to make bread. In the morning they looked at grains and considered the role of grain within an economy and looked at the historical development of different grains around the world. Then they set to grinding some and then they started baking. Baking was treated as a science lesson, they experimented with chemical reactions and learnt about live cultures and how they work, they also experimented with the physical properties of an oven and temperature and they looked at the biological impact of bread as a food source upon the body. All day long the top three year groups worked together, mixing, kneading and baking and every child brought home their own loaf of bread. It was so delicious that it barely lasted till tea time. This was in a primary school where they have greater flexibility with how they run their school day or their curriculum.

Contrast it with my older son in secondary school. In the first year his cookery lessons seemed to be all about assemblage. Create a salad, create a fruit salad, design a sandwich. It was not edifying. This year he has been allowed to approach the ovens but not for long. Every offering that the poor boy has brought home has been undercooked. You can see his frustration as he comes in and tells us not to bother eating it as he had to take it out before it was ready. It's maddening but the way I look at it is that at least he knows it's undercooked. I'm not impressed with the current secondary education system and the fact that my sons are currently having to go through it makes me even more unimpressed. Which is why I try to get them involved in as much cookery as possible at home. The problem is I may end up killing them first.

And a bad week

It's been a challenging week here at Hurley Towers. We made the decision to close the shop for November whilst Mevagissey gets its streets dug up. Trade is always weak in November so we thought this would be the perfect time to take a rest, get the scaffolding up, sort out the gutters or hanging gardens as they are more commonly known and get the shop painted. A bit of a spring clean ready for the Christmas lights and the launch of EV Thompson's new book. We knew that it would mean that takings for November would slump a bit but it's the best time of the year to do it. And of course we always have the internet sales to rely on….

As you can probably tell things haven't quite gone according to plan. Our neighbour discovered two hidden fireplaces in his walls and a rubbed out chimney – we had a day's panic whilst we thought we may have the same issue on our side but that seems to be a bill we have sidestepped. Just good old regular gutter damp. So there we were relying on the internet when I woke up to an odd e-mail. The customer asked, if I removed the free shipping would I be able to reduce the overall price?

That was odd? I left in it my "to do" pile and then opened another e-mail. This one just said "Are you kidding?" The next customer explained that they were short of funds this month but would I accept a round £5 million pounds for the Jack Higgins paperback? A sense of awful foreboding settled around me. Quickly I flicked to my online accounts and was astounded and then horrified to discover that I was pricing over half of my online inventory at over £1 million an item. So far the most I was asking for was £7.5 million for a Danielle Steele second hand paperback.

I had a quick laugh, replied to all queries and shouted to Steve that we had a mild hitch and that we were going to have to close all online sales whilst I tried to find out what was going on. About three hours should do it. It's now two weeks later and our software providers are tearing out their hair whilst trying to sort out the problem. We have no hair left to pull out as we have gone bald through the stress of it all.

We are making some sales but our prices are in a complicated mess. We had been joking that all we needed to do was sell one of those multi million pound books and all our problems would be solved. After day two that joke began to pale. So now we are looking at each other and asking how this could happen in the run up to Christmas? January and February is when we pull our belts in, not November. November is when I buy presents, plan Christmas menus and sort out who will be sleeping where when the family arrives. At this rate we'll be telling the children that Christmas Lunch is their present and yes Christmas Lunch this year will consist of fish and chips! If they're good we'll throw in the ketchup.

Hey ho. I know we'll get things fixed but isn't it frustrating when you think you have everything all worked out and then all of a sudden, it's all out of your control and you're spiralling rapidly towards a nightmare and wondering what possessed you to buy a new sofa. Oh and my cold has come back so I really am not impressed with my lot at the moment. Roll on next week, surely things will be better then?

How do we carry on when the world is so awful?

Sorry about last week's column, it did come across a bit grumpy didn't it but there's a point where you are feeling ill, your children are ill and your pets are ill that things just get on top of you. There's a point when just burning the toast makes you feel like bursting into tears at the unfairness of the universe. And then you switch on the news and hear how someone walked into a school and shot a bunch of little children and your own concerns come crashing down around your ears. Then I did weep because how can we live in a world where that happens? How can you kiss your child goodbye in the morning and never see them again. How can someone think that the way to solve their problems is to walk into a school and kill a bunch of children? How many people actually need to own an assault rifle? The Americans know they have a gun problem but they do nothing about it time after time, pleading the second amendment

221

like it's some sort of sacred cow. The fact that their constitution used to allow slaves and restricted voting to certain men shows that the constitution can be changed. In fact instructions were included in the constitution on how to make changes. Do they not understand what "Amendment" means? Their founding fathers knew that nothing was static and that changes would come and go.

As I sat there thinking about all of this I thought about how rubbish, futile and fake all of this seemed to me. I was no less grief stricken when I watched Dunblane or Columbine but then the days passed and their grief and tragedy faded into other minutiae of modern life. Thinking further I realised that this was just 20 children, what about the hundreds that die every day through war and poverty. Where were my tears for those children, where were the TV stations and journalists camped outside their parents' homes? Is it because the scale is too large to deal with? Because death of children is inevitable in drought stricken countries? What makes the death of one child more important than the death of any other child?

All extremely depressing but I think that is what makes the human spirit so indomitable. We are surrounded by tragedy every day, sometimes we hear about it, sometimes we don't, mainly it never affects us directly, occasionally it does but we persevere because how could we do otherwise? If we allowed ourselves to be overwhelmed by life, we would just stop.

So if I have a new year's resolution it will be to carry on as before. I am an optimist because there is too much in this world to feel awful about so it's easier and better to be hopeful. I wish you all the very best will in the world and hope that life is good to you and when it isn't, that you are able to cope. I promise my next column will be full of cheer. After all my whole family will have just been staying for a week what could possibly go wrong?

We all stand together

What is it that makes our winter events seem more community focused than our summer ones? In July and August, the banners are flying, everyone is in flippy skirts and pretty sandals, although I think Steve should shave his legs if he's going to wear his skirts that short! And everyone is looking their finest. The sun shines down from a bright blue sky, well, not usually but you get the picture, and the air is warm and beautifully fragranced with summer flowers. Hundreds gather, crowds throng and maybe you pick out a few faces you recognise amongst the visitors but in winter it's so very different.

Typically it's dark so we can ignore the looming clouds, it doesn't matter what we wear because no one can see us, so we are spared Steve's legs! and we are all looking at the same thing. In summer our eyes dart everywhere as there is so much to see. In winter we are all looking at the fireworks, or the bonfire, or the torchlight procession. We are all doing the same things standing alongside our neighbours, or our team mates or our friends.

So far we have come together to watch a beautiful fireworks display at St Austell Brewery, every year they generously invite all their neighbours and employees to come along and ooh and ahh. The following evening we went to an even more fabulous display and bonfire at the Lankelly Fowey Rugby grounds. Fund raising events like this one mean that we can add more bits of kit and start to save towards proper loos. Definitely something we mothers are looking forward to.

We have watched our children lead the Remembrance Day assembly as they struggle to come to terms with the fact that so many have died over the years only a few years older than themselves. A week later we watched them again raising money for Children in Need as they understood that suffering is not just a thing of the past or something remote. We were all a bit humbled when watching one of the videos, one of the school children, let's call him Jack, turned round and asked the adult what the name of the boy in the film was. No one could answer; we had all been focusing on the child's problems whereas Jack had instantly focused on him as a fellow human being. From time to time we may get "compassion fatigue" but children never do. They cut straight to the heart of it; they don't care about the politics, the social situations and the blame game. They just see that a child like them, a child who could be their mate, is in trouble.

We have also been wowed by the lantern displays in Truro but thrilled to see just how great St Austell's was. This is the rebirth of something very fresh and optimistic and long may it continue. Looking ahead we have the carol services and the Christmas lights to enjoy, when communities again come together in the darkness to celebrate. It always seems a shame that January and February seem to be devoid of these occasions, by then the long months of darkness and rain have begun to take their toll and we need something to keep our flagging spirits going. In the meantime though I'm going to make the most of all the upcoming events and make merry with the wassail and the egg nog.

228

A day in the life of a Mevagissey bookseller

Well it starts as always with a box full of books in the car and a drive in from St Austell. Today was hellishly windy but as I dropped down into the village the wind seemed to die down, clearly Heligan was taking the brunt of the winds. I drove down Jetty Street parked up and unloaded. This is always a tricky effort but easier in winter, this morning I am unimpeded by any other traffic and I drive off to park at the lighthouse. I could park in one of the other car parks, but I love walking out by the sea, dodging the seaweed strewn road and the splashing waves. It's also the cheapest place to park, which helps.

Walking back to the shop I'm stopped by a couple in a car who ask me if I'm local. Now there's a question. I doubt there are many other places in the world where such an innocent sounding question is laden with problems. No, I'm not local, I come from St Austell but even there I'm not local, I used to live up country, worse yet my parents aren't local either, neither are their parents. However, these guys are on holiday and just want to know if the Wheelhouse serves breakfasts. As if to underline how much of a local I'm not, I don't know the answer. Frustratingly the wife pipes up "Only we saw people in there eating breakfast…" Grrr, well surely that answers your own question!? On I stroll and pause to watch a cormorant sunning himself on a rock and think about how gorgeous life is sometimes, so long as you choose not to focus on daft questions.

The day progresses along normal lines, as we have the new E.V. Thompson title in, lots of people are popping by to collect their copy and all of them stop to share a story with me. They are really entertaining but I'm not getting anything done. Some people wander in for a browse and find some book that they can't do without. Others baulk at £3 and point out that they can get it for a pound at their local car boot sale. Hmm, off you go then.

Out in the street the wind is picking up but unfortunately for the Mevagissey Lights Committee this is also when they need to hang the new lights. Jetty Street is getting some amazing strands of lights running the entire length; they are going to look stunning. The lights committee are swearing as the lights refuse to switch on but the wind is whipping away any offending words and only the gulls are assaulted by the words and God knows they've had worse directed right at them.

By three the heavens open and the road is white with bouncing rain. By four I have my ark built and head home, I stop at Kim's to buy some fish and have to laugh. She was telling me when it started to rain she was chatting to some of the fisherman who promptly bolted at the first drop. Now there's a group of men that you'd think wouldn't melt in the rain. Then again, I should imagine that they have to put up with more than their fair share at sea. Getting wet inland is just too much. The road outside the fire station is flooded but there are people out helping to direct the traffic through the shallowest section. And then I'm off home again, driving out of Mevagissey and thinking about what a great day it's been despite the atrocious weather.

Next year I want a boring year!

"And so my friends, the time has come, for me to face the final curtain…" the end of the year always seems so dramatic doesn't it? We're asked to look back at what went before and to look forward and to consider what might be. There are times when it seems to sway between some sort of mystical balancing act and a business de-briefing but quite honestly what happened this year will pretty much be what will happen next year. Did you know the Chinese have a curse that says "May you live in interesting times" It doesn't sound like much of a curse until you consider that "interesting" is what makes it to the newspapers and TV. Floods are interesting, as are earthquakes, fire, death and disaster, quite frankly we may be interested to read about it happening to others but we certainly don't want to experience it firsthand.

Lots of interesting things have happened this year that I don't want to repeat, ever and quite frankly I don't think

I've "grown" from the experiences, nor has it "made me stronger". It was difficult, frustrating, boring and upsetting but as each thing happened we dealt with it and we got on with it. And before you think I had some major disaster in my life this year, I didn't, just the normal run of daily tribulations that we all cope with.

Of course some of us will have had wonderful things happen this year. Marvellously interesting things (interesting is a bit of a double edged sword) from the news of a new baby to the launch of a business, a slew of excellent exam results, a first job, a successful interview, a trip across Africa, the finishing of a house, all of these things are wonderful and are rarely ever going to make it to the news but they are what sustain us and keep us going whilst the other interesting things trip us up and pull us down.

So next year, a balance of interesting things please. Can the things I know about happen successfully and can the things I don't know about please not happen at all. It might make for a quiet year but I think that would be rather nice. And as for resolutions, well I want to take a photo everyday, I got as far as January last year, I'd like to get this column in on Wednesdays every week and not panic like an errant school girl on Thursday evening and finally I'd like to dive more.

I love diving which might surprise the people I dive with as they probably don't know what I look like anymore. For those of you who have ever thought that diving abroad looks fun, it is, but it's just as good here. Yes, I'll grant you that it's colder and the visibility is more temperamental but what we have, metres off the shoreline is wonderful; a whole hidden part of Cornwall, always quiet, never crowded and always beautiful. If it sounds tempting, make it your New Year's resolution to give it a go.

So that's my New Year's resolutions, what will yours be and how far will you get? I wonder how many people actually make a resolution and stick to it. Sometimes I think it's easier not to make any in the first place and then you won't feel that you've failed when you do fail. However, I also think it is worth the effort and one year I might actually succeed!

Have You Read...

SCRIBBLES FROM THE EDGE

The first collection of essays from Liz Hurley. If you liked this lot then you'll love the other book as well. Currently available from Hurley Books in Mevagissey, or on Amazon as a paperback or a kindle.

http://www.amazon.co.uk/Scribbles-Edge-Liz-Hurley/dp/0993218008/ref=tmm_pap_title_0

GIVE US A REVIEW....

In order to keep this book selling it needs lots of great reviews on Amazon or Good Reads. Good reviews help heighten the visibility of our books and allows more people to see them on their list of recommendations.

KEEP IN TOUCH...

We're on all the usual places, choose your poison and come and join us.
www.facebook.com/mudlarkspress
www.twitter.com/mudlarkspress
Instagram: and_then_it_exploded
https://uk.pinterest.com/hurleybooks/

LOOK OUT FOR MORE GREAT BOOKS FROM MUDLARK'S PRESS COMING SOON...

Mudlark's Press

Mudlark's was established in 2015 in a response to the nightmare of getting my first book published. In the end it seemed easier to do it myself, and whilst it actually wasn't easy at all, it was fun. Coming soon are a book of walks, a guide book and a children's storybook. After that? Who knows? Maybe you have something?

Mudlark is a family nickname and it felt nice to bring it out into the light. We have nothing to do with the Thames!

Printed in Great Britain
by Amazon